Praise for *Growing Disciples Organically*

Don Detrick understands the challenges of spiritual development in depth and takes his expertise to the pages of this book. He has a gifted way of explaining organic discipleship and development. His stories provide great context in practical applications to walk with Jesus. You'll enjoy this book tremendously.

DR. WAYNE CORDEIRO, bestselling author; senior pastor and founder, New Hope Christian Fellowship, HI

It appears that we have, for some time now, equated 'largeness' with success, when the real indicator has always been, for any fellowship, a transformed reproduction of one's faith. In *Growing Disciples Organically,* Don Detrick is on to something very unique and intriguing. Just as a beautiful plant can grow from a single seed, think what might happen to all of us if the 'seed' from this book takes root in our lives.

DR. H.B. LONDON JR., president, H.B. London Ministries; pastor to pastors emeritus, Focus on the Family

From his experiences in farming and ministry, Don Detrick is uniquely qualified to take us back to our spiritual roots. In *Growing Disciples Organically,* he explains that discipleship today has become too rigid, programmed, and scheduled. He shows how spiritual formation is the natural (actually, the *supernatural*) result of authentic faith, spiritual nutrition, and a rich environment of love and acceptance. Don takes the confusion and mystery out of the process by providing clear biblical insights, inspiring stories, and practical suggestions. I recommend this book to every church leader.

DR. GEORGE O. WOOD, author; general superintendent, Assemblies of God USA, Springfield, MO

Growing Disciples Organically digs deep into the gnawing challenge confronting churches and leaders alike: What does it really mean to follow Jesus in the 21st century? Using his own family upbringing and pastoral experience, Don Detrick provides keen discernment on spiritual formation that goes beyond a veneer of "slick" to the heart of the eternal matters facing every human being. If you are ready to stop long enough to take seriously the call to follow Jesus, *Growing Disciples Organically* may provide you a moment of keen insight that gives you new confidence on your spiritual journey.

—DR. BYRON KLAUS, president, Assemblies of God Theological Seminary, Springfield, MO

Spiritual growth is a complex process that is too often portrayed as the end result of following a cookie-cutter recipe. Don Detrick shows why program-driven and one-size-fits-all paths to discipleship don't produce the fruit we hope for. Better yet, he shows what does work—a model of spiritual formation that has far more in common with organic farming than assembly-line manufacturing. If you want to grow disciples, this book is for you.

—DR. LARRY OSBORNE, pastor, North Coast Church, Vista, CA; author, *Accidental Faith*

Some explorers enthuse over their exploits with "You should have seen what I saw"; others return with a map. New ideas about church can sound exciting, but without a map very few of us will make the effort to travel. Don Detrick is a spiritual cartographer. This book is a map to a new kind of church. Don's map shows us how to travel from where we are as a church to where he thinks we ought to be and still get back home alive. Who knows, after a couple of trips, you may decide to move there permanently.

—JIM HENDERSON, author, *Jim and Casper Go To Church* and *The Resignation of Eve*

Very few people have the combination of deep spirituality, sparkling intellect, and people-oriented practicality that Don Detrick has. In *Growing Disciples Organically*, he combines real-life farming experience with all of the above to offer a no-nonsense approach to making disciples of Jesus Christ. Deep enough for academic or church use and real enough for personal appropriation, this is the best book I've read on making disciples.

—DR. JOSEPH CASTLEBERRY, president, Northwest University, Kirkland, WA; author of *Your Deepest Dream* (NavPress, 2012)

Growing Disciples Organically is a great read, a true page turner. Detrick contemporizes New Testament principles of church growth. Not a book presenting steps or methods, but a very engaging application of what Jesus taught. So many pastors and leaders are searching for the next "big idea," yet missing the organic growth principles of Scripture.

Bob Schmidgal founded Calvary Church, Naperville, Illinois with a few people and some college students. He was our pastor when I served as president of the National Association of Evangelicals. One day I asked him why he didn't join the hundreds of pastors traveling to Pensacola, Florida to be part of the revival taking place there. His response was so simple. "God called me to pastor Calvary Church. He will give direction for what we need to do to reach this community." When Bob died in his early fifties, attendance averaged over

4,000. Although he never read *Growing Disciples Organically*, his leadership reflected the exact concepts Detrick presents. This book is a must read for all pastors and leaders.

—**DR. DON ARGUE,** chancellor, Northwest University; former president,
National Association of Evangelicals

If you are done with step-by-step, processed Christianity and want something that feels more authentic, Don Detrick's *Growing Disciples Organically* is for you! Don looks at the teachings of Jesus through the lens of his background growing up on the farm, providing great insights on homegrown, nutrient-rich, unpolished disciples.

—**WES DAVIS,** lead pastor, Newlife.TV Church, Silverdale, WA

Growing Disciples Organically is a refreshing and truthful book, because it details the authentic experience of growing disciples. Having served in churches as a pastor, as well as having assisted pastors for many years, I have grown weary of quick-fix methods for discipleship and, for that matter, of quick-fix methods for growing a healthy church.

Don Detrick has highlighted the truth that spiritual formation is a very personal experience with our Creator and His truth. As disciples, we are connected to the real (not synthetic) Lord. Growth takes time, and as we grow we become healthier and stronger as the character of the Lord becomes part of us. We are formed much like a seed, which is transformed into a seed provider. Detrick, who grew up on a farm, uses the metaphor of farming, including soil preparation, planting, growing, and finally experiencing mature plants—which, in turn, produce seeds to start new plants. This is very similar to our spiritual formation experience: organically produced, connected to the real Jesus, and developing into disciples who are healthy and able to reproduce our faith in others, so they may begin their spiritual journey with Christ.

—**DR. WAYDE GOODALL,** dean, College of Ministry, Northwest University,
Kirkland, WA; author.

We can't change anyone, but we can mirror Christ's method of spiritual formation in developing others. Don's literal farming roots give a fresh perspective on growing disciples. A must read for those truly intent on nurturing growth in others.

—**TRACEY C. JONES**, author; president, Tremendous Life Books

Don Detrick reminds us that growing disciples has more in common with fields than factories. Field work is hard work, but Don's book *Growing Disciples Organically* prepares us all to be soulful, Master-like gardeners.

—CHAD HALL, MCC, director of coaching, Western Seminary, Portland, OR; co-author of *Faith Coaching: A Conversational Approach to Helping Others Move Forward in Faith*

As I read Don Detrick's book, I found myself repeatedly saying, *"Yes! Yes!"* Detrick writes from years of experience as a church leader, pastor, and Christ-follower. He reminds us in this powerful book that, too often, we in church leadership miss what is real and true. Could it be that we are using the wrong measure for success in church growth? Using the metaphor of organic farming, Detrick describes what it means to be a real, down-to-earth follower of Christ. Every pastor and church leader—anyone who longs for real success in the church—will want this book.

—NANCIE CARMICHAEL, MA in spiritual formation; bestselling author and speaker

It's true. I'm biased when it comes to this writer since I've shared marriage, ministry, and life with Dr. Don Detrick for almost four decades now. But that gives me a distinct advantage when it comes to knowing the character and the heart behind the words of this book. Don's love to see healthy growth—whether in the bonsai plants and roses he has tended through the years, or the people he has nurtured as a caring pastor and spiritual leader—is authentic to the core. In *Growing Disciples Organically: The Jesus Method of Spiritual Formation*, you won't find some slick, step-by-step 'how-to' for easy, cookie-cutter discipleship. But you will find wise, biblical insights to encourage you as you partner with the Master Gardener in growing lives (both your own and others) to look more like Jesus. I love this book and I love its author!

JODI DETRICK, columnist for *The Seattle Times*; national chairperson for the Network for Women in Ministry

Growing Disciples Organically

The Jesus Method of Spiritual Formation

DON DETRICK

Published by
Deep River Books
Sisters, Oregon
www.deepriverbooks.com

ISBN-13: 9781937756819
ISBN-10: 1937756815

Library of Congress: 2013933695
Printed in the USA

Cover Design by David Litwin, Purefusion Media

Contents

Foreword

If you see a book online or lying on a coffee table that bears the name of an author you know personally, you are far more likely to pick that book out of the pile, open it, and read it. The first time I heard that illustration was with reference to the Bible. I was receiving instruction as a young person on how to become a more developed and devoted follower of Jesus, a better disciple. My mentor accurately stated that the more familiar I became with the author of the Bible, the more inclined I would be to read his Book. Perhaps he did not recognize how truly organic and profound his words were, but he was right. In my lifelong pursuit of becoming a more devoted disciple of Jesus, I have indeed recognized that my hunger to hear God's Word is proportionate to the depth of my relationship with him at any given time. This is but one of many life lessons that have informed me that discipleship is relational, it is cyclic, it is perpetual. In a word, it is organic.

I know Dr. Don Detrick, the author of *Growing Disciples Organically: The Jesus Method of Spiritual Formation,* and I know him well. Everything I know about him as a person and as a leader causes me to embrace his timely work on a vital topic. Dr. Detrick is first and foremost a fully devoted follower of Christ himself, and he demonstrates this consistently in his personal and professional life. Don is a *disciple.* He has also demonstrated over years of time his ability to *make disciples*, and he does so in just the way he illustrates and promotes in this volume, organically. I have come to recognize, with considerable interest and delight I might add, that much of his ability to lead and disciple others is rooted in his youthful experiences living and working on a farm. I never tire of his childhood reflections about life on the farm. Those experiences were truly organic to his formation, and he successfully draws upon that knowledge and experience to offer keen insights into what it takes to make and grow disciples today. Just prompt Don to reminisce about his first paid job as a fertilizer vendor (chicken manure to be exact), and you readily see how his formative youthful experiences on the farm helped shaped Don into the wise and practical leader he has become. (Let's be honest, much of our time as a leader is spent in effectively "managing manure," an insight I wish I had been given much sooner in life and ministry!)

If you were to gather Christian leaders from across America, or even the world, and allow them to engage in a free-wheeling discussion on issues of greatest concern to them in ministry, the topic would inevitably turn to discipleship. Leaders are challenged by the task. I was in a recent national meeting of denominational leaders where it was boldly stated that "growing healthy and productive disciples of Jesus is both the most important *and* least understood task facing church leaders today." Leaders are looking for discipleship insights and approaches that produce lasting fruit, but struggling in the application of methods that are at least out-of-date, if not demonstrated to be ineffective. Most of us would confess to the irresponsibility of leading a person across a line of faith in Christ only to fall short in our effort to grow them into Christ as a productive disciple. We must recognize this as nothing short of failure to complete the Great Commission of Jesus to "make disciples of all nations," which in Christ's own words is comprised of baptism, learning, and obeying (Matthew 28:19). This historic directive of Jesus must be embraced as our contemporary responsibility and embraced from the organic perspective Dr. Detrick has so capably articulated.

We live in a time when modern approaches sometimes clash with what we have come to know as postmodern perspectives. The modern approach taught me to see discipleship as a linear process, with a well-defined scope and sequence. Modernism taught me to view discipleship through the lens of prescribed catechisms, with starting and ending points that are clear and predictable. Discipleship was deemed successful when adequate doses of biblical and theological knowledge had been

dispensed in order to help a prospective disciple "arrive" at an educational or informational destination. In many cases, we even felt that this
task could be completed in a detached or rote fashion, without the com-
plications and intricacies that are inevitably encountered in a true relationship between the disciple and the disciple-maker while "doing life
together."

Yet, our review of Jesus as a disciple-maker affords a far more organic
process, and one that is arguably more postmodern in character. The discipleship of Jesus was more relational and less informational. It was less
linear and more abstract, seizing upon opportune moments to initiate
growth and change in his followers. Jesus allowed the disciples to unfold
what God set before them rather than always unfolding it for them. For
Jesus it seemed as much about the journey as it is about the destination.
It was not nearly as prescribed and predictable as we would like to make
it for our own convenience, and we know it wasn't convenient for Jesus.
As I have heard it so appropriately described, "Discipleship is messy." So
is farming the organic way, but the ultimate harvest is one that is healthy,
attractive, and savory.

If you devour this book, you will surely learn something significant
about its author and his own organic formation as an Oregon farm boy.
More importantly you will be afforded insights on organic discipleship
that parallel the Scriptures, and reflect the discipleship approaches of
Jesus himself. We live in an hour when healthy and productive disciples
of Jesus are desperately needed, and we must seek every legitimate means
to produce them in response to the command of Jesus.

Les Welk
Superintendent,
Northwest Ministry Network
of the Assemblies of God

Preface

Perhaps this has happened to you. You open your Facebook homepage and discover a dozen requests from friends asking for a few baby chicks or some seeds to start a crop or garden. Some days I think if I see, "Want to trade a cow for a milk goat?" one more time, I will just cancel my Facebook account. Thankfully, privacy settings have allowed me to block most such requests for the present.

Okay, I'll admit I'm really not an online gamer anyway, so my aversion to Farmville comes as no surprise. What surprises me is the public fascination with virtual farming. Growing up with dirty hands, muddy boots, and smelling of manure-caked jeans, my recollections of farm life have nothing in common with sitting in front of a screen playing a game with the aroma of freshly brewed coffee in the air. The business of farming requires physical labor and emotional commitment coupled with a realization that hands-on participation is required, not optional.

Anyone who has done it knows that growing things is hard work, not a game. So it is with growing people, as any parent or educator can tell you. The laboratory of life provides the necessary ingredients, and when mixed with appropriate quantities of love, grace, and discipline, a person learns and grows through a process that can be as organic, smelly, and messy as changing a baby's dirty diapers.

In much the same way, growing disciples best takes place the way Jesus did it—in the field of human existence, while rubbing shoulders with other people. You may think becoming a disciple of Jesus Christ is best accomplished by sitting in a church building or classroom while listening to a lecture on some biblical topic, or by reading a book. But is it possible that scenario is far from reality, sort of like playing a computer game about farming compared to the real sights, smells, and activities of agricultural life?

To those who observe trends, the Farmville mania was part of an important shift and movement in this second decade of the twenty-first century. I will write more about it in chapter one, but for now it is important to note that people far from the environment of farm life are becoming fascinated with foods and how they are grown.

"Certified organic." The words create either a warm, positive response from the consumer willing to pay a little extra for produce bearing the seal (or a harsh, cynical response from those who view the organic label as a bogus marketing ploy). Either way, both would probably agree we are in the midst of an organic whole foods revolution, and the believers seem to be gaining traction as evidenced by the rise of organic grocery chains like Whole Foods Market. Anything organic captures attention these days, with the promise of organically produced commodities leveraging an ever-larger market and ever-increasing cohort of enthusiasts.

---

or·gan·ic (ôr-gàn′îk)

1. Of, relating to, or affecting organs or an organ of the body: *an organic disease.*

2. Of, relating to, or derived from living organisms: *organic matter.*

3. (a) Using or produced with fertilizers of animal or vegetable matter, using no synthetic fertilizers or pesticides: *organic gardening; organic vegetables.* (b) Free from chemical injections or additives, such as antibiotics or hormones: *organic chicken.* (c) Simple, healthful, and close to nature: *an organic lifestyle.*

4. (a) Having properties associated with living organisms. (b) Resembling a living organism in organization or development; interconnected: *society as an organic whole.*

5. Constituting an integral part of a whole; fundamental.

6. *Law.* Denoting or relating to the fundamental or constitutional laws and precepts of a government or an organization.

7. *Chemistry.* Of or designating carbon compounds.[1]

Living in the Seattle area, I've observed this phenomenon and been amazed at how eagerly the Puget Sound public embraces anything organic. Menus in some of the most high-end restaurants in the area feature organically grown, locally resourced foods. Anything labeled organic, locally raised, and sustainable is in high demand and commands a premium price.

I sometimes have to chuckle at this trend. As a boy growing up on the farm, "city slickers," as we called them, seldom expressed an interest in anything homegrown, homemade, or rural unless it was to laugh at the bumbling country antics of *The Beverly Hillbillies* on television. On the other hand, with the exception of bananas and a few other commodities, if we didn't raise it or grow it ourselves, we did not eat it. Now, being a "hick" is hip, at least when it comes to your palate.

A recent article in the Seattle Times addressed the growing organic and whole foods movement:

> We're fed up with the fake, the fast and filthy. We want it slow, and we want it real. First 5,000 years, almost everybody is a farmer. Last 50 years, nobody is a farmer. Last couple of years: Everyone wants to be a farmer. Or hug a farmer. Or at least buy and eat local food that isn't sprayed, injected, modified, adulterated, and transfatted into inedibility.[2]

When it comes to definition number three above, organic is going mainstream. There are many reasons for this; some will cite health concerns, while others tout the benefits to the environment. What this means from a practical standpoint is that agriculturalists are discovering new and innovative ways to grow massive quantities of fruit, vegetables, grains, and even livestock using a different set of tools to enhance production as opposed to those discovered and used in the twentieth century.

The modern age gave us the ability to mass produce enough food to serve the hungry throngs in growing urban and suburban population centers. To do so required all the mechanics and chemistry of the age of industrialization. Advances in science gave us machines and irrigation options that enabled us to cultivate vast tracts of formerly unproductive or arid land. It also gave us the chemicals to make fertilizer for faster and enhanced growth, and pesticides or herbicides to eliminate most of the diseases, weeds, and pests always lurking nearby to destroy the crop.

The organic revolution in many respects represents a postmodern backlash against the modern age of industrialized, consumer-driven, and corporate-farm styles of agricultural practices. Advocates possess an almost religious adherence to certain core values, promoting a greener-earth philosophy and environmentally friendly practices. Many truly believe that a shift to organic could prevent global warming and help save the planet. While I personally find that a bit of a stretch, I readily concede the sincerity of those thus persuaded. Organic agriculture symbolizes more of an ethos, or a cultural shift, than simply a preference or appetite for different foods on the menu. In this case, the palate is not the tongue, but the heart and mind, reflecting the soul of individuals who feel the need to shift to organically produced foodstuffs.

These philosophical platitudes generate strong emotions among both organic promoters and detractors. The tension is palpable and readily felt through exposure to any form of media in today's culture. I personally do not believe organic farming is such an either/or question (as there are rational arguments and reasonable people on both sides of the fence). However it is easy to see the prominent place organic concepts play in today's version of culture wars. But, you may ask as you remember back to the title page of this book, "What does all this have to do with spiritual formation?"

Actually, it is possible to see many parallels with organics and the current tensions between traditional and emerging streams of evangelicalism.

Younger generations are discovering that bigger churches do not guarantee spiritual formation in the life of attendees, nor do they equate greater numbers with greater levels of spiritual passion or vibrancy. Seeking what they have been missing, many are opting for simpler structures, more focused on community and interpersonal relationships. For some it means a return to more liturgical or ancient forms of spiritual expression; for others it means joining a house-church movement. And a growing number are leaving the established church behind altogether.

Might today's implosion of corporate structures parallel at least the gradual demise of the institutional, denominationally based church growth witnessed during the twentieth century? Is it possible that both the corporate world and evangelical denominational organizations are facing the same need for restructuring to evaluate their true mission and adherence to core values and purposes? Might the passing from the scene of evangelical icons like Billy Graham signal the end of mass evangelism crusades, at least in North America, and a return to simpler, "viral" relationships as a means for bringing people to Jesus and promoting spiritual formation? Might our growing observation that program-driven mega-churches seem to have a life span directly correlating with the life span of the founding pastor be changing our focus away from that particular model of church growth or spirituality? Do we really believe that discipleship should have a shelf life?

In *You Lost Me*, author David Kinnaman describes why young Christians are leaving church and rethinking faith. He states, "Many are searching for new ways to be effective in their work with this new generation, and many are waiting for the next generation of leaders to emerge. Among these groups, there is a growing sense that we need new ways of discipleship, a new way of teaching, instructing, engaging, and developing the lives of young people. We need a new mind to focus on apprenticeship in the way of Jesus."[3]

Apprenticeship precisely describes my experience growing up on a farm. I was there, I participated in life, and I learned. Having been both a pastor and a farmer, it has been my joy over the past thirty years to serve congregations numbering from a few parishioners to more than a thousand. There are many parallels in both vocations. I studied modern agricultural methods in high school while serving as president of our local chapter of the Future Farmers of America, and studied the Bible, theology, and ministry in Bible College and seminary. My insight into growing things was not gleaned from reading a slick magazine on gardening or organic farming, but from getting my hands dirty with the sweat, soil, and manure of everyday farm life.

The melding of my two vocations has served me well over the years and provided insight about the way things grow, both in the physical and spiritual realms. I would suggest that the things leading to spiritual growth do not require a degree in theology to understand, although I possess a few of those. It seems to me that the basic components of spiritual formation, or what we often call discipleship, are fairly simple to understand and readily available. How do people really grow, spiritually speaking? Using the model of Jesus and his disciples, I notice that the process did not require any of the staples of modern notions about discipleship: curriculum, buildings, schedules, or programs. As I read the Gospels, they portray the entire three-year process as far more organic and fluid than programmatic and structured. And from what we see in Acts and beyond, it certainly must be sustainable with the enablement of the Holy Spirit.

Using the model of Jesus in the Gospels, growing disciples seems as natural a process as watching a child grow into maturity. Didn't Jesus specifically instruct us to consider the qualities of children as a model for his kingdom? Based upon that model, organic spiritual formation describes a vision for discipleship, or growing disciples organically. Simply put, it involves the components of faith, life, and community. Here is a working definition:

Organic spiritual formation

The natural growth that occurs when authentic faith in Jesus Christ is merged with intentional alignment to the principles of Scripture and empowered by the Holy Spirit, while living with and serving others.

FAITH

Authentic faith in Jesus Christ is the primary component of organic spiritual formation. The writer of Hebrews tells us, "And without faith it is impossible to please God, because anyone who comes to him must believe that he exists and that he rewards those who earnestly seek him" (Hebrews 11:6). Faith is the predominant theme of the New Testament and a subject Jesus often addressed. Yet faith is not the same thing as certainty, and there remain many mysteries about faith that must be explored and dealt with by followers of Jesus. Jesus referred to faith as a seed, and seeds are meant to sprout and grow.

LIFE

A seed can appear to be a dead and lifeless thing until it sprouts to life. To produce organic spiritual formation requires a life committed to Jesus Christ—that sprouting seed of faith going from death to life. This leads to obedience to his Word. It is impossible to do this in our own strength. No one was capable of total obedience under the Old Testament law and no one can earn salvation by obeying rules assembled from New Testament texts. Growth occurs as we align ourselves with Scripture by consciously receiving the grace of God through the power of the Holy Spirit.

COMMUNITY

More apples exist in a single seed than there are seeds in an apple. Seeds multiply. So does living faith. In order for spiritual formation to occur, our faith and life must be lived out in a community environment. The Great Commandment involves loving the Lord first and loving our neighbor as ourselves. If faith does not work while living with others, and if it does not compel us to serve others, then we will not witness significant spiritual growth. I invite you to explore these topics in detail as we proceed in the next chapters.

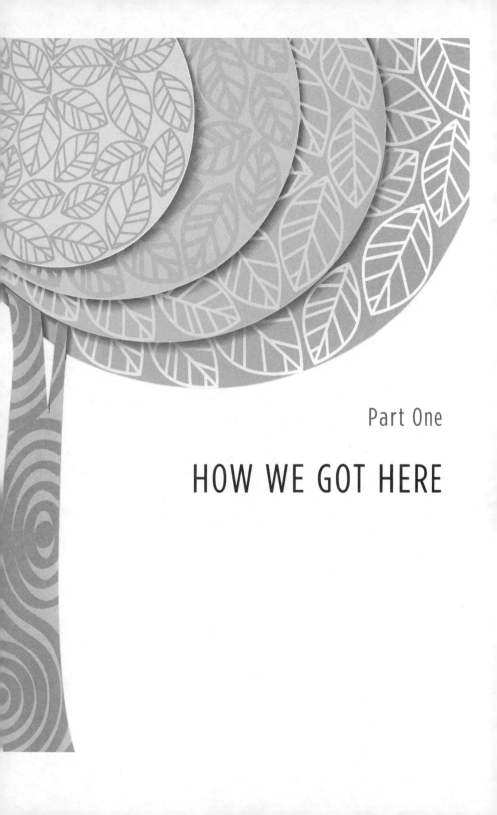

Part One

HOW WE GOT HERE

Introduction

"Over my dead body!" The other board members felt the tension mounting in the room, but were not prepared for Pete's vitriolic emotional outburst. "My family has attended this church for three generations and paid for much of this building. What you are calling for won't make this church grow; it will drive the final nail in the coffin! If we could just get back to old-fashioned preaching, evangelistic meetings, and singing like we had when Pastor Jones was here, we'd have real revival and we wouldn't be able to contain the crowds. If you'd listen to me, I could tell you what works. We need children: puppet ministry, a good Sunday School contest, or a big event like the Sunday School conventions we used to attend—that would really bring them in."

Pete's outburst left him red in the face and out of breath. The rest of the board seemed stunned and unable to verbalize a rational response to Pete's irrational diatribe. Discussions about declining attendance and shrinking budgets had dominated the agendas at Clearwater Community Church board meetings for the past year and a half. Tonight's agenda was no exception. Simplistic solutions such as those proposed by Pete had already been discussed ad nauseam. Others had proposed dramatic changes, like selling the building, cutting staff, or trying to restructure to attract a completely different audience.

Chagrined, Pastor Jason was about to respond with, "Pete, if you liked Pastor Jones so much why did you help orchestrate a coup to have him voted out years ago? And why don't you just do us all a favor and move back to the 1950s if you enjoyed living there so much?" He caught himself before he verbalized those acrid thoughts. There was enough

3

tension in the room already; he didn't need to exacerbate the situation. But Jason had taken just about all he could take. The lack of spiritual maturity and vision from board members like Pete seemed incomprehensible. "Surely Clearwater Community Church is not the model Jesus had in mind when he said, 'I will build my church,'" he mused.

Although fictional, the above scenario is a composite representation of similar situations I have witnessed over the years in my experience as a pastor, consultant, and denominational executive. While much of the above conversation concentrated on the topic of church growth, it begs to ask broader questions: What if we discovered the missing ingredient in our quest for church growth? And what if that missing ingredient had more to do with individual spiritual growth than the numbers shown on annual church reports? Would we be having the same conversations?

I have met a lot of people like Pete in my travels and usually their motives and intentions are exemplary. But they often subscribe to a narrow view limited to their own parochial version of reality and spirituality. Rather than reflecting creativity and diversity, or a willingness to embrace change when necessary, members of Pete's gang default to entrenched positions, sacramentalized by their own nostalgic view of the past and the way things ought to be from their point of view. The notion that there might be different methods or means of "doing church" that include changing schedules, music, or programs seems dangerous to them, even heretical.

To paraphrase Jesus (Mark 2:22), the old wineskins that church members such as Pete have carried and treasured for so long are not able to withstand the pressures that are involved in changing to new methods with the wine of new generations. As Jesus said, new wineskins are necessary for new wine. Explosions seem inevitable as the old wineskins burst from the pressure. The resulting collateral damage usually serves to alienate older members from the very ones who might provide the spark of life, leading to the growth they truly desire. Is it possible that demanding to have things their own way might be an indication of their own lack of spiritual maturity? Let's explore this a little further.

We'll begin by taking a look at the status of discipleship in the American church in the next two chapters, which will be of particular interest to pastors or church leaders. If you are more interested in getting right into practical steps for organic discipleship, feel free to skip ahead to chapter three.

At the end of each chapter you'll find questions for further individual or group study. These are designed to help you create a conversation about the concepts presented in the chapter, and I hope that they will help you discover practical next steps to assist your own spiritual growth.

At the end of the book (following the afterword) pastors and church leaders will discover reflection questions. The questions are not intended to be a comprehensive manual, but a means to kick-start a conversation. They should facilitate honest dialogue among the members of leadership teams about the state of discipleship in their local church and help them collaborate in new ways to grow disciples organically.

CHAPTER ONE

A Spiritual Health Examination

A s unlikely as it seems, in the opening months of the second decade of the twenty-first century, an online agricultural community had become the number-one group of gaming enthusiasts on Facebook, topping more than sixty-nine million members. Farmville residents live off the virtual landscape and parlay their holdings in farmland, livestock, and commodities to become virtual participants in a way of life reminiscent of a bygone era. Along the way, Farmville players learn skills in agricultural practices, business management, and community. Since the disappointing initial late-2011 stock offering of Farmville's parent company, Zynga, enthusiasm for Farmville has waned. Enthusiasm for all things organic has not.

Like Farmville, at one time in the United States the Grange was a powerful organization boasting more than a million members between the 1890s and the 1950s. From its beginning in 1867, the Grange encouraged farm families to band together for their economic well-being. Over time, the local Grange Hall became the political and social center of rural communities across America. Grangers (as members are called) were influential, and helped shape America by lobbying for free rural mail delivery, forming public utility districts to bring electricity to all Americans, and fostering legislation to break up the railroad monopolies that stifled economic potential.

Eventually, the Grangers' efforts were so successful that transportation became affordable over great distances. In 1872 the first mail-order catalog was sent by Aaron Montgomery Ward, one page in length, listing a hundred and sixty-two items. By the mid-1880s, the catalog was more than 200 pages long and sold 10,000 items, allowing people in rural areas to access anything city dwellers could buy—from farm implements to jewelry, furniture, musical instruments, books, or clothing. Montgomery Ward and Sears, Roebuck and Company became mega-corporations by offering a vast inventory of products available to all through catalog mail-order sales. The same factors led to cheaper agricultural commodities, local grocery stores, and eventually supermarkets. The Grangers' success in their political endeavors actually contributed to the urbanization of America—and the eventual downfall of their own organization.

A few years ago, the local Grange in my community closed its doors. The remaining Grangers were in their eighties and above, and with no younger members standing in the wings to assume leadership, its fate was sealed. What took place in my local community of North Bend, Washington is typical of local Grange outposts across America. North Bend was once a thriving agricultural community. Today most of the farms are gone, and it is a suburb east of Seattle known as an upscale community—a great place to raise families for employees of nearby Microsoft or Boeing. Nintendo has a major production and shipping facility next to our factory outlet mall.

The contrast between Nintendo and The Grange is a picture of our community context and; in a broader sense, of the realities in the modern and post-modern worlds. One organization has geared itself to provide cutting-edge technology to engage and entertain children and adults. The Grange seems dedicated to nostalgic memories of the past and preserving a way of life that for the most part does not exist anymore. Nintendo aficionados are a growing tribe of children and young families. Grangers' ranks are populated by senior citizens and diminishing in number. Which do you think will be sustainable throughout the twenty-first century, Wii or Grangers? Which organization would you buy stock in?

However, one local Grange is not only surviving, but thriving. Through the intentional efforts of a new generation of Grange leaders, new members are regularly recruited in the unlikely setting of upwardly mobile Woodinville, Washington. The Grange Master is thirty-six years old and successfully engaging younger members and families by providing a place of community and affinity that fits the community context. But it required some creative changes organizationally to make it happen.

When Clark, the Woodinville Grange Master, started with the organization in 1997, "He found the organization intriguing. It was active in political and charitable work. But he thought the meetings were arcane and cloaked in meaningless rituals. There was the 7½-minute opening, for starters. Members sang three songs and marched; the secretary read aloud *all* of the correspondence. Seventy years ago, there was nothing better to do than listen to a four-hour boring meeting," he said. "The problem is that society changed, but the Grange didn't."[1]

At least one early Granger saw it coming. Albert Goss, past master of the National Grange, wrote in the 1930s:

> The question has been asked, "How long will the Grange live?" I believe it will live as long as it continues to serve the welfare of agriculture and the nation. Whenever it becomes ingrown and selfish, and the members look on it only as a means of bringing them pleasure, entertainment or profit, it will fade away.[2]

It doesn't require a detective to examine the evidence and notice the similarities between what has happened in the Grange movement and what is currently taking place in the organized church in America. When I first read the words of Albert Goss spoken more than three quarters of a century ago, I thought, "He could be speaking about the church today!" For many churches and members, like Pete mentioned in the introduction, organized religion has become ingrown and selfish. Our consumer society feeds the idea that church exists for whatever the individual needs or wants. That is exactly what makes Rick Warren's opening statement in *The Purpose Driven Life* so poignantly powerful, "It's not about you!"

As I write on a Sunday afternoon, I've just read this headline in the Sunday paper *Parade* magazine: "Has America Become More Spiritual?" The accompanying article cites a recent poll that affirmed that Americans are interested in spirituality—in fact only 5 percent of those surveyed identified themselves as "atheists." Of the respondents,

45 percent identified themselves as "religious," but 70 percent of all respondents said they participate in "organized religion sporadically or not at all."[3]

Though *Parade* magazine is hardly known for its stellar research, its survey findings are not surprising. For years research and opinion polls have told us that Americans are open to spirituality as individuals, but increasingly closed-minded toward organized religions. For most, the gap between the individual (the organism) and the church as a whole (the organization) is increasing. There are many reasons for this, but among the most prominent cited is the casual observation that there is often a *disconnect* between beliefs and behaviors among members of organized religions, specifically within the Christian church. This is precisely why the concept of organic spiritual formation could prove useful in engaging the masses who are open to spirituality, but not organized religion.

An organic view of spiritual formation acknowledges that seekers need space to explore faith and contact with followers of Jesus before crossing the line of faith or making a decision for Christ. It also acknowledges that twenty-first century seekers often value belonging before becoming. When given the space and time to grow, spiritual formation occurs.

THE REVEAL STUDY

Back in 2004, leaders of Willow Creek Community Church published the findings of a commissioned three-year scientific study (using both qualitative and quantitative research) to examine not just the attendance or giving patterns of church members, but also their spiritual formation. The resulting Reveal survey took a deeper look at the hearts, disciplines, and spiritual maturity of more than 5,000 active congregational participants from seven different churches. Data was collected and analyzed with surprising, if not shocking results. Based on research results, the connection between church activity and spiritual growth appears to be limited. This revelation prompted the title, *Reveal*, and the following chart shows part of the revelation:[4]

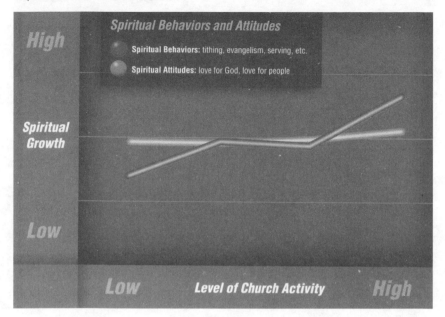

An advertisement for the book documenting the results states:

Numbers can be helpful, but they don't reveal the whole story. Numbers can't peer into the human heart. When it comes to spiritual growth, we need to be able to measure more than numbers. We need a glimpse of people's attitudes, thoughts and emotions. We need a tool that reveals the heart of each person. *Reveal* promises to offer such a tool, based upon the results of the survey.[5]

So, what were the surprising results of the research? In a nutshell, the findings definitively showed that there is no direct correlation between spiritual formation and local church participation. Conventional wisdom expects to discover a direct linear relationship between the level of participation (active membership, volunteerism, participation in activities, tithing, sharing resources, etc.) in a local church and that person's spiritual maturity. *The Reveal Survey*, which has since been used with thousands of congregations and hundreds of thousands of participants, clearly shows that no such relationship exists. This is alarming because it indicates that the typical metrics for measuring the effectiveness of a church—attendance numbers, conversion/baptism numbers, or financial numbers—really do not translate into Christ-like character, or what many churches see as their primary mission: "To develop and equip fully devoted followers of Jesus Christ."

Much has been written about the Reveal study, including the sequel, *Follow Me*, and recently released follow-up, *Move*. All three resources have provided useful data over the past decade to draw the conclusion that spiritual formation does not automatically take place by simply attending church, or even by active participation in church-related activities. The bottom line of the study declares that spiritual formation can be viewed and even analyzed on a continuum that identifies four stages of the spiritual journey:

- Exploring Christ
- Growing in Christ
- Close to Christ
- Christ-centered

In *Follow Me*, the authors note the two key breakthrough discoveries that most clearly signify spiritual formation. These will be discussed further in this book. First, "Christ-centered people show enormous capacity for increased kingdom impact." Second, "The Bible is the most powerful catalyst for spiritual growth."[6] Whether these are "Aha!" factors or "Duh!" factors, depends upon your own perspective. Regardless, they represent the best research on spiritual formation, and in the following chapters we will look more at these results as components of organic spiritual formation from an individual perspective.

Move is the latest book in the ongoing Reveal study on spiritual growth. In it, authors Hawkins and Parkinson offer simple advice based upon statistical research for four best-practice strategies common to churches that are highly effective in growing disciples by moving people closer to a Christ-centered model. They show that people progress across the spiritual continuum in three movements: early spiritual growth, intermediate spiritual growth, and advanced spiritual growth. Moreover, they show that "individual spiritual growth is not linear or predictable, but a complex process as unique as each individual, and it progresses at a pace determined by each person's circumstances and the activity of the Holy Spirit."[7] In addition to expanding upon their original research, the authors detail the frustration experienced by many believers in their stalled or nonexistent spiritual formation.

A Spiritual Continuum Emerged from the Research

Exploring Christianity

"I believe in God, but I'm not sure about Christ. My faith is not a significant part of my life."

Growing in Christ

"I believe in Jesus, and I'm working on what it means to get to know him."

Close to Christ

"I feel really close to Christ and depend on him daily for guidance."

Christ-Centered

"God is all I need in my life. He is enough. Everything I do is a reflection of Christ."

They offer practical suggestions for measuring a church's spiritual vitality index and list four best practices for growing disciples revolving around Christ-centered leadership. First, churches serious about spiritual formation and discipleship get people moving by providing accessible entry points and understandable and practical strategies for growth. Second, they embed the Bible in everything they do. Third, they create ownership and help believers understand they don't just *belong* to the church—they *are* the church! Empowerment of individual disciples and helping them take responsibility for their own spiritual growth is a priority. And finally, these churches don't just view themselves as a part of a community, they view themselves as on a mission to pastor the community.[8] In somewhat different terms, we'll talk about the organic components and application of each of these practices later in this book.

For the moment however, let's consider the health of the corporate evangelical church in America. With all the opportunities for publishing, media, and education afforded us in the current era, we ought to be better equipped than any generation in the Christian church. If advances in technology, transportation, and communication were the means to spiritual formation, then we should have at our disposal the tools for creating the most strategic discipleship initiatives in the history of the church. Sadly, the facts deny this:

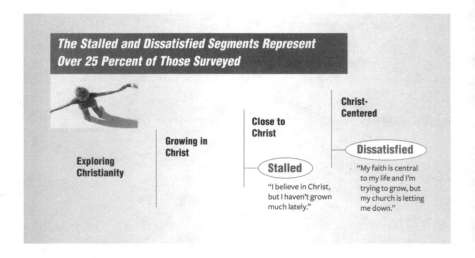

WHAT WOULD IT TAKE TO CHANGE?

Let's revisit Pete from our earlier example for a moment. What if Pete's comments and attitudes better reflected the life and purposes of Jesus Christ, rather than a time-warped, culturally irrelevant version of his own local church back in the glory years? Pete loves the Lord, but is that reflected in his heart toward people in his own community who are not like him? Is it represented in his lack of willingness to make room for younger leaders or accept change gracefully if it means leaving the security of his comfort zone?

What would it take for Pete to change? Is it too late? The same question could be asked of churches across America. In the church I serve,

known as one of the fastest growing denominations in the twentieth century and beyond, we have many young people in our congregations. But
retaining them as adults is challenging. When it comes to ministers, we
have more over the age of sixty-five than under the age of forty. Only
14 percent of our nearly 12,000 congregations in America are served
by lead pastors under the age of forty.[9] Thankfully, we are intentionally
engaging younger ministers in a strategic effort to change these dynam-
ics. The rationale for doing so is even more compelling as 2010 census
data points to growing ranks of baby boomers as a percentage of population, and a shrinking number of those under twenty.

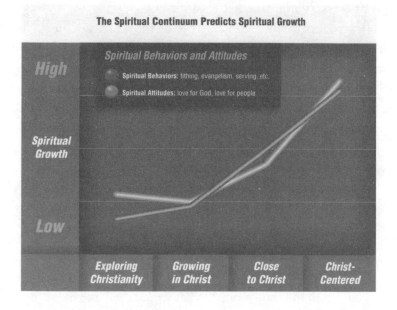

Spiritual growth behaviors are linked to spiritual attitudes, the
greatest of which are love for God and love for people—obedience to the
"Great Commandment" according to Jesus. I don't want to be too hard
on Pete. The truth is, Pete and his generation are passing away. Likewise,
my boomer generation cohorts are losing influence as emerging generations take the reins of leadership. In January of 2009, for the first time
in my lifetime, the President of the United States was a person younger

than me. President Obama's election centerpiece consisted of a message of change and engaging younger and more diverse constituents. And pundits believe his re-election by a wide margin in 2012 reveals affirmation of the change and diversity he represents. The church cannot neglect the potential ramifications of that same message and hope to survive in its present institutional form.

The future of the church lies not so much in engaging members of Pete's generation as in engaging younger generations and members of unreached people groups to become fully developed and committed followers of Jesus Christ. How will that happen if we are unwilling to take a serious look at our own methods for evangelism and discipleship and fail to make necessary adjustments?

My purpose in this book is not to debate the veracity of the arguments either for or against organic methods, or even the modern vs. postmodern or traditional vs. emerging church controversies. Rather, I hope to simplify the basic components of spiritual formation in a way that is both understandable and reproducible. Surely this is possible, but it requires taking a deeper look at who we are, where we are, and how we got here.

FOR FURTHER PERSONAL OR GROUP STUDY

1. A quote from this chapter states: "There is often a disconnect between beliefs and behaviors among members of organized religions." Has that been true in your experience, and if so, why? What might be done about it?

2. Look at the first chart in this chapter. Where do you see yourself in the continuum? What would it take to move forward in your faith and spiritual formation?

3. Many people in the Reveal study cited in this chapter indicated they were stalled or dissatisfied with their spiritual growth. What could that indicate, and what do you think is the solution?

4. Another quote from the chapter states: "The future of the church lies not so much in engaging members of Pete's

generation as in engaging younger generations and members of unreached people groups to become fully developed and committed followers of Jesus Christ." What do you think about that statement? If you are a part of a local church or community of faith, how does it apply to you or your group?

5. Discipleship is often linked to spiritual disciplines such as prayer, Bible study, scripture memorization, meditation, silence, solitude, sharing your faith, etc. How are these elements taking place in your personal life or faith community? What else is needed to grow your faith?

6. Considering where you are in your faith walk with Jesus right now, where would you like to be, and what would it take for you to get there?

CHAPTER TWO

How Is It Working for Us?

M y father was born in 1916 in a sod house on the prairie of eastern Colorado. His father was a Dunkard Brethren elder (minister), born in 1857, and like most ministers of his affiliation, earned his living by tilling the soil. Widowed while in his fifties, grandpa re-married to my grandmother, a single woman in her late thirties, and started another family. I was born nearly a century after my grandfather's birthdate, seven and a half years after he died at the age of ninety. I grew up on the same farm in the Willamette Valley of Oregon my father moved to in 1927 at the age of ten. That was when his father, who by then was seventy years old, purchased the property.

In his early years, dad plowed many furrows of land with a team of horses and a single steel plowshare. When he had earned enough to buy his first tractor and two-bottom plow, he got rid of the horses and never went back to the old ways of farming. He had entered the modern age of agriculture. Had he not bought the tractor and incorporated innovative methods, he might have prayed more, tried harder, worked longer hours, and been more committed than his neighbors, but they still could have out-produced him simply because he was using the old technology.

The older I get, the more nostalgic I become about life on the farm. In reality, I often hated it as a kid. I longed for blacktopped driveways on which to ride my bike and play basketball. I loathed the mud and manure of the farm, and the aromas that went along with it. The older we get, the more we glamorize the past because we have more memories of the past than potential for the future. Annoyed by change and longing for the "good old days," we remember them as being much better than they really were.

Generationally, we can look at the same thing from a very different perspective. When I was a boy and I looked at the old horse tack, collar, and harness hanging on the barn wall, I thought of Roy Rogers, becoming a cowboy, and riding into the sunset on Trigger. When my father looked at the same objects, he saw a lot of hard work and effort that he had long since traded for the modern convenience of a tractor. Before I was born, Dad had already sung "Happy Trails" to the horses and, for him, it was a good riddance.

My father lived on and worked that same farm for seventy-five years, until 2002 when he died. He lived long enough to pay off more than one mortgage and to see many changes in agriculture, including what I would call "postmodern" agriculture, the currently lucrative organic product market. In many respects this represents a re-packaging of the way we did things before modern agricultural methods, but with a slightly different twist because of twenty-first-century environmental and health concerns.

I cannot help but see similarities between my family's experience on the farm and the organizational challenges facing the evangelical church in the twenty-first century. In three generations my family went from the premodern, to the modern, to the postmodern age. The evangelical church has endured the same transitions, but many forms of evangelicalism are still stuck organizationally and operationally in the modern age. Even more alarming, if the truth were told, many of the churches I am familiar with have not fully embraced the modern age. Some are suspicious even of computers and video technology in the church. They seem happier clinging to their premodern ways, feeling somehow more secure and even more spiritual by using a hymnal rather than reading the words from a screen, to use one common example. In the meantime, they cannot understand why their children or grandchildren constantly have an iPad, tablet, Nintendo DS, Kindle, or netbook in their hands yet seem disinterested in spending even an hour per week at their church.

THE IMPORTANCE OF VISION

How do we envision the future of the church? How well does that vision incorporate spiritual formation or discipleship? What will happen when the builder generation leaves the scene of the local church? I believe these are crucial questions as we enter the second decade of the twenty-first century. The rapid influx of change in the past two decades makes it difficult for any of us to prognosticate the future too much beyond next week.

As the people of God, our heritage is in the past generations of the church of Jesus Christ; church history and tradition should not be ignored. But we cannot live in the past. We should have learned by now that every generation needs a new experience with God in a way that is both biblically based and culturally relevant. Evangelicals love to look wistfully back to events like the Great Awakening in the early eighteenth century, or the Second Great Awakening in the late eighteenth and nineteenth centuries. Pentecostals view the Los Angeles Azusa Street revival beginning in 1906 as a watershed moment that ignited the Holy Spirit's flame across America and around the world. Yet longing for the past or wishing for the good old days does nothing to improve the spiritual climate of the current era. It can, in fact, be an indicator of organizational mortality, because when our memories of the past are more exciting than our vision for the future, we have begun to die.

We make the best presentation of the Gospel in language that is understandable to the listener. Instead of leveraging this new opportunity to reach younger generations or new people groups moving into our communities, churches often tend to isolate themselves from those who are different, not feeling the missional need to learn the language of the new inhabitants or present the Gospel in a way that fits their current community context. That seems odd, because those are the very things we pay career missionaries to do when working overseas, and missions represent a concept readily embraced by those who are most traditional. So instead of engaging the culture, while embracing God's purposes, some choose to cling to their nostalgic niches and hope that they can hold on till the end—in the meantime vilifying anyone who disagrees with them or does not see the beauty in their objects of affection, be those objects buildings, musical preferences, specific versions of the Bible, or style of preaching.

WHAT ARE WE MISSING?

In fact, it is this tendency toward polarization that may have robbed us of viewing spiritual formation from a more holistic viewpoint and integrating it into all aspects of life, rather than relegating it to an hour per week of Sunday school, or some other programmatic approach. Let me explain. In my role as a denominational leader, I spend most weekends visiting or speaking in different churches. As you might imagine, there is great variety, even within my own denominational context. And though some would vehemently deny the allegation, most churches do appeal to a certain market within the evangelical world. This is often observed by the particular emphasis of the local church, most generally focusing on insider issues rather than on those outside the church. Here are a few examples:

- *First Church of Biblical Information.* In this church Pastor Edgar Expounder specializes in verse-by-verse expository teaching and preaching of the Bible. Everything else pales in comparison to that forty-five minutes on Sunday morning. He can attract a good-sized audience, notebooks and Bibles in hand. Spiritual formation is expected to occur in this church by listening to sermons and memorizing verses from the Bible.

- *First Church of How to Do It.* This is similar to the First Church of Biblical Information, with less emphasis on the biblical information aspect and more emphasis on the "how to" practical approach. Pastor Helpful Howard specializes in applying the Bible to life topically instead of verse-by-verse, and he actually uses "steps" rather than "points" to develop his messages. Members of the First Church of Biblical Information tend to think the members of the First Church of How to Do It accept a "watered-down" Gospel because Pastor Howard does not share a biblical proof text for every paragraph of his message, but sometimes uses object lessons or video clips to illustrate the steps in his message. Spiritual formation is expected to occur in this church by following Pastor Howard's six easy steps or three hard ones.

- *First Church of Signs & Wonders.* Pastors Ken and Barbie Renewal project a youthful image and are dressed in snazzy attire. They are quick to encourage guests to expect an exciting time during the service. They are also quick to claim that revival is on its way, or soon would be if only God's people prayed more, worked harder, gave more, got out of the way and let God have his way, or just stopped listening to those ever-prevalent "Jezebel" spirits. Spiritual formation is expected to occur in this church by transforming experiences, as a result of fasting and prayer.

- *First Church of Wealth & Success.* Pastor Given Moore sports a Rolex, wears a designer suit, and drives a BMW. He looks and sounds like a Fortune 500 CEO, and his parishioners look like they could be his army of blue-collar workers. In exchange for their sacrificial offerings, he offers them the chance to name and claim for themselves whatever they want—and backs it up with lots of cool stories and an occasional Bible verse. This congregation seems to be the most in flux as people are constantly rotating through the front and back doors—at first enamored by the promises of prosperity, but soon disillusioned and heading out the back door. In this environment, marketing is key to a steady flow of new customers. Spiritual formation is expected to occur in this church by planting seed (giving money) and experiencing the resulting blessings.

- *First Church of Required Relationships.* Pastor Rogers wants everybody to have a neighborhood to call their own, and you must join a small group or two to become a member. Introverts usually don't stick around long, because they are called upon to speak or read in front of the group from the first meeting on. For the members of this church, spiritual formation occurs by applying the "one another" passages of the Bible to everyday life.

- *First Church of Social Transformation.* "We're out to change our world" is the mantra of Pastor Bill Goodwill. Under his leadership, this church is known for their good works and building bridges in the community. Members of the other churches in town accuse Pastor Bill of preaching nothing but a "social gospel," although they have a hard time faulting his church's impact in the community and his knowledge of the Bible. Spiritual formation is expected to occur in this church by doing good works and promoting peace and justice.

- *First Church of Doctrinal Purity.* Pastor Theo Logic often directs visitors to the statue of John Calvin in the courtyard of the church. His sermons and tracts lead you to believe that the corner on the truth is located within the four walls of their very own building. Spiritual formation is expected to occur in this church by study and through the ability to categorize life events within a doctrinal system.

- *First Church of Perfected Principled People.* Pastor Lester Perfector wants the church code of conduct printed in the bulletin every week, not just on the visitor cards. After all, some people might forget the rules of membership, which include acceptable behaviors such as how many children a submissive wife should bear, proper attire for every activity, or medical procedures every true believer should avoid. His motto is "we strive to be holier than anyone else." Spiritual formation is expected to occur in this church by following the rule, "practice makes perfect, and nobody's perfect, but we have to keep trying."

- *First Church of Programs for Everyone.* Pastor Perpetual Motion wants everybody to feel at home and offers a program for every need. This requires a demanding schedule for volunteers, but busy people are seldom lazy people. Mention a need to Pastor Motion and you'll be drafted to fill it. Pastor Lester Perfector often compares this church to a stream a mile wide and an inch deep. Spiritual formation is expected to occur in this church by activity and learning on the job.

Although written with tongue firmly in cheek, I suspect those with much exposure to the evangelical church in America can easily identify one or more of the churches I just described. The humor of the situation is tempered by the realization that many adherents in these congregations are led to believe that their model of church life, or style of worship, or spiritual disciplines or distinctives, are the most important components of a life dedicated to the service of the Lord. Pastors often cite commitment as the definitive key to spiritual formation. Many parishioners believe most sincerely that if they just stay involved in church as committed participants, they will grow. Instead, they may find themselves burned out, apathetic, or resentful of those who seem to experience blessing without exhibiting their own self-perceived level of commitment. There must be better ways and means of spiritual growth.

FOR FURTHER PERSONAL OR GROUP STUDY

1. A quote from this chapter states: "As the people of God, our heritage is in the past generations of the church of Jesus Christ; church history and tradition should not be ignored. But we cannot live in the past." How would you describe your spiritual heritage, and what, if any, effect does it have on you today? What are the dangers of living in the past?

2. Why do you think some people cling to traditions? What are some good traditions that you hope to keep?

3. This chapter talks about vision. How might a compelling vision of what it looks like to follow Jesus help people grow in faith?

4. What do you think about the "tongue in cheek" examples of churches in this chapter? How would you describe the ideal church?

5. "Many parishioners believe most sincerely that if they just stay involved in church as committed participants, they will grow." Do you agree or disagree with that statement? How do you think people grow spiritually?

CHAPTER THREE

Organic—Framing the Picture

W hat does organic spiritual formation look like? How does faith begin to take root? To gain a clear perspective, we must take a look at the frames we use to view the actual picture. When we take a look and observe how Jesus interacted with his disciples, we must be careful that we do not frame the picture with our own twenty-first century Western-world mindset.

For example, the pages of the Gospels provide many compelling images of Jesus, yet we are never provided an actual physical description of Jesus beyond Isaiah's vision of a suffering Messiah (Isaiah 53) and the Gospel writers' details about the events leading to his crucifixion. What pictures come to your mind when you think about Jesus? Is he short or tall, bearded or clean-shaven? Could you identify his ethnicity? Do you see him as a shepherd or as a lamb? How about a preacher, a leader, or a carpenter? Do you see him as a son, a brother, a friend, a thirty-something man walking on water? Would your picture of Jesus portray him as harsh or compassionate? Would he be smiling or frowning?

One thing is certain, the pages of the Gospels do describe how Jesus took a motley crew of blue-collar workers from a variety of occupations and backgrounds, and spent three years training, mentoring, coaching, and equipping them to do the most important work in the history of the world—to launch the church of Jesus Christ. Along the way, they often failed to meet expectations, and most, like Peter, failed the final exam.

But in the end, Jesus handed them the keys to the kingdom of God and empowered them to take it from there.

Remember that the dictionary gives seven different definitions for "organic." The word is multifaceted. In the same way, looking at spiritual formation, particularly in the context of the gospel accounts of Jesus and his disciples, is also multifaceted. A closer look at the definitions for organic indicate that the word has to do with growing things, a holistic perspective involving people, laws, and organizations.

Organic spiritual formation defies a simple definition. So rather than trying to define a simple term that will fit into our box, let's expand our box a bit and imagine that organic spiritual formation encompasses a number of factors or frames for several different boxes. Each are as unique as an individual's DNA, but with characteristics that can be applied to all people in all places at all times. Because it might be easier to know what we are not talking about first, let's explore a few of the frames that might fit our view of the picture, but that don't necessarily fit into an organic view.

WHAT ORGANIC SPIRITUAL FORMATION DOES NOT LOOK LIKE

I think it is fair to conclude that the ways and means Jesus used to equip and empower his disciples look somewhat different than the methods we have come to rely upon to grow disciples or prepare people for ministry. After all, do you know of any local church or denominational body that would consider ordaining a man like Peter, who had very little if any formal education along with a few significantly noticeable character defects? Would they allow him to preach a sermon to a crowd of thousands just a little more than a month after publicly cursing and denying that he ever knew Jesus? I think we both know the answer to those questions. So, again we must examine our frame of the picture by taking a look at some other frames that won't fit. Organic spiritual formation doesn't look like a tract or pamphlet titled *7 Steps in 7 Days for Following Jesus.* Do we really expect that a person will be transformed in a week's time into a fully developed follower of Christ by reading a twenty-page tract? I do not question the intrinsic value of books, tracts, pamphlets, devotional literature, and audio or video resources to assist discipleship.

But organic spiritual formation requires more than just handing a person a piece of literature or DVD and expecting spiritual transformation or formation as the result. Historians tell us that pamphlets were the primary means of obtaining social or political change for nearly three centuries leading up to the current era. This is perhaps nowhere more evident than in the formation of the United States of America. From Tom Paine's *Common Sense*, to *The Federalist Papers*, to Ben Franklin's *Poor Richard's Almanac*, the printed page proved that in the end, the pen is indeed mightier than the sword. In the nineteenth century, Bible, missionary, and tract societies seized upon the popularity of print and growing global literacy. Their publishing efforts helped spread the Gospel throughout the world.

The invention of new forms of media in the early twentieth century significantly changed methods of communication and marketing. For example, a recent Library of Congress exhibit indicated that posters reached their peak of impact during World War I. Images of Uncle Sam recruiting soldiers and selling war bonds were everywhere, before radio or television advertising had been thought of.

While the printed page survived and thrived after that, Christians were also quick to seize the opportunity to use the phonograph, radio, television, and films as a means of spreading the Good News, opening new avenues for cultivating evangelism and spiritual growth among the masses. At the close of the first decade of the twenty-first century, newer forms of technology are making twentieth-century methods of communication obsolete. During this time of unprecedented change, we cannot hitch our horse to one particular form of technology or communication and expect it to take us where we need to go into the future as the primary means of spiritual formation or growth. You may be reading this as a traditionally printed "tree book," or as an e-book on a variety of devices, and all are equally effective.

Nor does organic spiritual formation look like attending a class, or sitting through a church service, or even attending a Bible college or seminary. While these may be important components in the life of a disciple, to paraphrase an old saying, "sitting in church doesn't make you a Christian any more than sitting in a garage makes you an automobile or sitting on the railroad tracks makes you a train." Unless the attendee has a dynamic relationship with Jesus and others, there is no possibility of organic spiritual formation, no matter how many classes have been attended, sermons heard, or degrees earned.

Organic spiritual formation doesn't look like an evangelistic crusade or revival meeting. Frankly, these were good tools that seemed to have reached their peak during the mid-twentieth century. They may still serve to enhance spiritual formation, and may be culturally relevant in some parts of the world, particularly for evangelism. However, as tools for spiritual formation they lack an audience or following in twenty-first century North America. This is a reality that needs to be faced by pastors and congregations who expect an occasional "revival meeting" or guest speaker to breathe life into their congregations.

At best, "revival meetings" provide a jump-start or CPR, but cannot sustain life or growth for long, and the reasons seem obvious. The conventional wisdom of twentieth century evangelical thinking was along these lines: "If you come to faith in Christ, you should drop all of your unbelieving friends because they might pull you down."

Then we would tell people, "We are having revival meetings, so invite all your non-Christian friends."

We should have listened when they said, "But you told me I couldn't have any non-Christian friends."

Instead we said, "Well, that is OK, just come and maybe you can bring some friends from another church and we'll have really good services. The Lord will touch you, and you will grow." For churches that use an annual or semi-annual "revival meeting" as their only model or means of spiritual formation, the question must be asked, "How is it working for you?"

Finally, organic spiritual formation doesn't look like marketing, door-to-door sales, slick advertising campaigns, or programs that promise more than they can ever deliver. Don't get me wrong, I am not among those who vilify the church for marketing strategies. Having been a pastor of a growing congregation, I know the importance of good business strategies and using effective means to reach seekers for Christ. What I am referring to is the programmatic approach to discipleship that promises spiritual transformation or formation by plugging into a church program. And I'm not against programs per se, but we must recognize their limitations and realize that Jesus did not come to enhance our programs, but to enhance our lives in an abundant, value-added way (see John 10:10).

You have heard the ridiculous claims made by TV marketers who prey upon the majority of us who want to lose weight. They say things like, "Have you ever said, 'I feel fat today,' or 'I wish I could still fit into my wedding outfit?' Millions of Americans just don't seem to be able to lose that baby fat around the belly, on the hips or thighs ... but now there is hope with Billy Bob's Belly Button Barometer. Unlike conventional weight loss products, you just stick this on your belly button and "presto" it regulates your inner metabolism—the fat burner we all have but haven't been able to tap into until now—to help you lose weight. Apply it today, and you'll start shrinking tomorrow!" Well, you get the point.

The sad fact is, those claims are no more ridiculous than those made by televangelists or even some pastors who entice their audience to give a "sacrificial love offering" in exchange for a blessed handkerchief, olive oil from the holy land, or healing water from the Jordan River—all with the promise of miracles or spiritual blessings. There isn't a miracle device that can help you lose weight, and there isn't a miracle object or program to increase your faith or help you become more christlike without any effort on your part.

WHAT ORGANIC SPIRITUAL FORMATION LOOKS LIKE

"OK," you may be saying, "so I have an idea what organic spiritual formation *doesn't* look like, but what *does* it look like?" They say a picture paints a thousand words, and I think the best way to describe it involves using a series of metaphors or word pictures to help frame the big picture and us see how the process looked for Jesus and his disciples. After all, aren't word pictures precisely what Jesus used to paint on the canvas of his listeners' imaginations? He used concrete examples, like building a house, to describe abstract concepts like faith, hope, and love. So let's step back to get a better perspective on how it might work for us as we grow in an environment of faith, life, and community.

FOR FURTHER PERSONAL OR GROUP STUDY

1. "What pictures come to your mind when you think about Jesus?" How would you answer that question?

2. Think about the disciples Jesus chose. What do you know about them? Did Jesus make good choices? How did they grow?

3. Review the section titled, "What organic spiritual formation does not look like." What part of that discussion did you most strongly react to? Did you agree or disagree, and why?

4. What do you think about the use of technology within the church? How could technology help promote spiritual growth? What are the dangers of technology?

5. Without reading ahead to the next chapter, what metaphors do you think work well to describe organic spiritual formation, or discipleship?

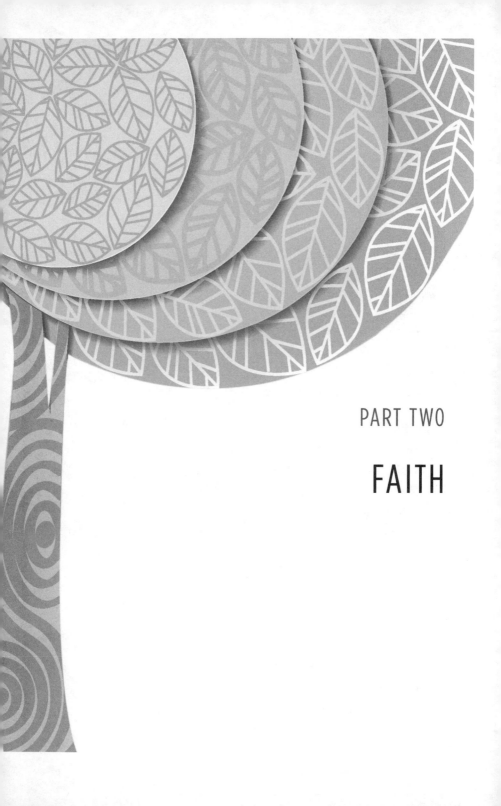

PART TWO

FAITH

CHAPTER FOUR

Basic Elements of Faith

I t all starts with a seed. At least this is true for most biological organisms. For purposes of our conversation, we won't worry much about asexual reproduction, cell division, and such. While those might serve as appropriate metaphors for organizational growth, we will stick with the basic facts of life. When it comes to producing a crop organically, seed is important. And faith begins with a seed.

I remember my Aunt Mary once asking my dad why his garden was so prolific while hers that particular year failed to produce much of a crop. Her corn, tomato, and cucumber plants in particular, which normally thrive in Oregon's Willamette Valley where we lived, looked somewhat peculiar and either failed to bear altogether or produced mysterious-looking vegetables that were virtually inedible. "Where did you buy your seed?" my father asked.

"Oh, I didn't buy any seed this year" replied Aunty Mary. "I saved money by saving my seeds gleaned from last year's crops." Aunt Mary was both thrifty and a good gardener.

"That's your problem!" replied Dad. "With today's hybrid vegetable seeds, you can't just save your seeds from this year's harvest and plant them next year. Not only will the hybrids fail to produce the same type of seed as the parent plant, you don't know what your plants were pollinated with, so the results will be a mystery and not very tasty. I don't really think you saved much money!" Because dad was always willing to share both his advice and produce, I'm sure Aunt Mary got some of both that year.

GROWTH FACTORS—BIBLICAL PARALLELS

Most of us learned about photosynthesis in elementary school science. We are familiar with the basic elements for growth of a living organism. They include the following: seed, sunlight, soil, water, light, air, and nutrients. When these are available and properly proportioned, they create an environment that makes growth automatic. Each of these has a biblical and spiritual parallel that we will explore in more detail in the following chapters. For now, I'd just like to list a few Scriptures that correlate with these elements:

- *Seed:* "For you have been born again, not of perishable seed, but of imperishable, through the living and enduring word of God. For, 'All men are like grass, and all their glory is like the flowers of the field; the grass withers and the flowers fall, but the word of the Lord stands forever.' And this is the word that was preached to you" (1 Peter 1:23–25).

- *Sunlight:* "When Jesus spoke again to the people, he said, 'I am the light of the world. Whoever follows me will never walk in darkness, but will have the light of life'" (John 8:12).

- *Soil:* "He also said, 'This is what the kingdom of God is like. A man scatters seed on the ground. Night and day, whether he sleeps or gets up, the seed sprouts and grows, though he does not know how. All by itself the soil produces grain— first the stalk, then the head, then the full kernel in the head. As soon as the grain is ripe, he puts the sickle to it, because the harvest has come'" (Mark 4:26–29).

- *Water:* "Jesus answered, "Everyone who drinks this water will be thirsty again, but whoever drinks the water I give him will never thirst. Indeed, the water I give him will become in him a spring of water welling up to eternal life'" (John 4:13–14).

- *Air:* "The wind blows wherever it pleases. You hear its sound, but you cannot tell where it comes from or where it is going. So it is with everyone born of the Spirit" (John 3:8).

- *Fertilizer/Nutrients:* "So he said to the man who took care of the vineyard, 'For three years now I've been coming to look for fruit on this fig tree and haven't found any. Cut it down! Why should it use up the soil?' 'Sir,' the man replied, 'leave it alone for one more year, and I'll dig around it and fertilize it.If it bears fruit next year, fine! If not, then cut it down'" (Luke 13:7–9).

IDENTIFICATION

Farmers and gardeners alike love to spend winter months poring over garden seed catalogs. Because of our familiarity with growing things, we generally learn to identify certain seeds early on. Of course, some seeds are more difficult to positively identify than others. Members of the same family, like cucumbers and melons, have similar seeds and it can be difficult to tell them apart. While you don't have to be an expert, a certain amount of knowledge in seed identification can avoid some disappointments at harvest time.

Hoeing and pulling weeds are basic gardening chores. But before sending one of my children to the garden for the purposes of conducting such an exercise, I always made sure we had a little lesson in identification at first. "Remember when we planted those corn seeds? Well, now this is what those little corn plants look like. We want to let them grow. Anything else can be considered a weed and removed."

Sounds simple, doesn't it? Over the years I earned the blisters and calluses from gripping a hoe often enough to prove that this exercise is not as simple as it seems. And despite my experience and technique, it is deceptively simple to take out a corn plant (or two or three) with the hoe right along with the weed. There are some biblical and spiritual analogies here, but we'll save them for later. The point is, if you are going to plant a garden, you must know what the plants look like.

And here is the rub: for most living things, the plant itself does not really look much like what the plant is being cultivated to produce. There are obvious exceptions—lettuce, spinach, rhubarb, and cabbage look like what they are—because we consume the leaves or stalks themselves. But unless you know what a corn plant looks like, you will not be able to identify it, because it looks absolutely nothing at all like an ear of corn. It might resemble a milo or millet plant, but it doesn't look like corn itself. The same is true for most orchard fruits. You simply cannot tell by looking at a tree if it is an apple or cherry or pear tree, unless you have learned to identify it by its leaves and branch structure. Only when it is bearing fruit can a non-expert identify it.

Identification is important because you must start with the right seed to produce the desired crop. Speaking prophetically as with the voice of God, Isaiah wrote, "It is the same with my word. I send it out, and it always produces fruit. It will accomplish all I want it to, and it will prosper everywhere I send it" (Isaiah 55:11, NLT).

Learning to identify the authentic helps you recognize a counterfeit or that which is not genuine. We may not always know if a person has authentic faith, but Jesus does. He said, "My sheep listen to my voice; I know them, and they follow me" (John 10:27).

WHAT ABOUT SPIRITUAL GROWTH?

I've already listed the primary components of organic spiritual formation: faith, life, and community. Again, here is my working definition of spiritual formation:

Organic spiritual formation:

The natural growth that occurs when authentic faith in Jesus Christ is merged with intentional alignment to the principles of Scripture and empowered by the Holy Spirit, while living with and serving others.

A few years ago, NFL running back legend Shaun Alexander, who also happens to be a follower of Jesus Christ, sent out this tweet of 140 characters or less on Twitter: "Everything is a seed. Every word, every action. Everything we do plants that seed. Every seed does bear fruit.

What kind of seeds do u plant?" Shaun poses a great question. What are we planting? Organic spiritual formation occurs when we intentionally plant seeds that will bring forth good fruit and bless others.

What are the signs of spiritual growth? The answer is surprisingly simple, yet we frequently discount simple answers, thinking that something as important as spiritual formation must require a complex equation of prescribed elements to be effective. It is precisely our "thinking" or cognitive part that often gets us into trouble. With our Western world mindset, we tend to view the solution to every challenge as a linear, step-by-step process. Our minds process most challenges in a step-by-step, formulaic process. Did you notice how many times I just used the word "process"? Spiritual formation involves a process, but not necessarily the way we think of a process. Let me explain.

CHIA PETS AND SPIRITUAL GROWTH

Suppose I ordered a chia pet online. On the happy day it arrives at my doorstep via UPS, I have trouble containing my enthusiasm when I pick up the package. As I unpack it, what do I expect to find? (Now to be truthful, I've never actually ordered a chia pet, but I've seen the infomercial enough to know what to expect.) I expect to find my own chia pet—maybe a dog or a pig would be nice. They are made of clay and I would expect it to arrive unbroken—that would be helpful. I would expect to find a little packet of seeds and maybe some glue-like soil stuff I would mix with water to make it stick to the chia. I'd also expect to find step-by-step, detailed instructions for how to do all of this written in twenty-seven different languages. Hopefully I'd find English among them. Finally, I would earnestly expect that if I followed all the steps, within a few days my chia would be experiencing the amazing transformation from a red, dead piece of clay to a green, living, and growing clay pet of my very own!

Growing spiritually is in a few respects like growing a chia pet, but in most respects it is nothing like it at all. John Ortberg writes in *Leadership Journal* about our tendency to formulate and program spirituality in measurable terms by means of a few spiritual disciplines such as reading the Bible or writing in a journal. He says,

Devotional practices are not the ultimate criteria for spiritual growth. In Jesus' day, the people who would have rated highest on devotional practices would have been the scribes and the Pharisees ("I thank you, God … that I fast twice a week; I give tithes on all I get"). But they were not examples of spiritual maturity.[1]

For many years my own pastoral experience led me to believe that the commitment level of my congregants was a prime indicator of spiritual maturity. I reasoned, "If people are committed, they will be involved in the ministries of the church and growth will be automatic." Many pastors hold a high view of commitment, and bemoan the lack thereof in today's church. However, Ortberg deconstructs that reasoning with some further insight on commitment as a measure of spiritual maturity:

> Sometimes churches measure spiritual progress in terms of commitment. Where would the Pharisees be by this scale? Far right. They win. Commitment was not the problem.
>   But consider another possibility. Jesus said the ultimate command was to love. Commitment is not the same thing as Christ-likeness. In fact, where people's primary focus is on their commitment, pride is not far behind. Where the primary focus is on Christ, commitment no longer seems like such a heroic thing. It just seems sane.[2]

While it involves a process, organic spiritual formation is more of a matrix than a linear step by step equation. A variety of components can be inserted into a matrix rather randomly, depending upon the circumstances and individual. It would be easy if it were a rubric or template, something like, "Decide to be committed to this, then attend church weekly for one hour, then five minutes of Bible reading daily, three minutes of prayer twice a day, and memorize one verse weekly." That kind of process is easy to quantify, prescribe, and measure. You either do it or you don't—you can mark the steps off on a chart or to-do list and be evaluated on the results. Unfortunately, those simple steps are not really a formula for spiritual growth. An atheist could follow the steps without a resulting change of heart. There must be more to it than a few easy steps. Again, I ask, what are the basic components of spiritual formation?

THE IMPORTANCE OF SCRIPTURE

Richard Foster, in his insightful book, *Life With God*, lists three components of spiritual transformation, "vision, intention, and means." When I read that, I first thought, "Here is a simple answer to my question." I appreciate Foster's contemplative insights and the legacy he has left the church regarding spiritual disciplines. However, as I read on, I discovered there is a lot more to what he is saying than just three simple components. What he describes is an ongoing process of spiritual transformation that occurs by reading the Bible—that is the focus of his book. However, it is not just reading, but reflecting, meditating, applying, obeying, and interacting with others about the Bible. In the resource section in the back of the book, Foster lists fifteen expressions of spiritual transformation within the people of God that he lays out in a systematic, but somewhat complicated chart. Though extremely useful, it is not something one could easily grasp or memorize for daily spiritual fortification when you are going through a tough time. That is not really its purpose anyway. The point is, though the basic components of spiritual formation are simple, the process can be anything but.

Foster rightly views Scripture, and our interaction with it, as a key to spiritual formation and transformation. To this end, he has also provided *The Renovare Spiritual Formation Bible* for twenty-first century disciples as a wonderful tool in the process of organic spiritual formation. It is only a tool, however, not a magic pill for spiritual growth. In addition, Foster illustrates one of the main points of the *Reveal Study*, that spiritual formation is tied to biblical knowledge and application.

JESUS AND SEED

It should come as no surprise then, that Jesus described Scripture as the key component, or seed ingredient, for spiritual formation. The writers of the three synoptic Gospels, Matthew, Mark, and Luke each tell

Jesus' story of the seed and sower (Matthew 13:3; Mark 4:3; Luke 8:5). We'll focus on Matthew's telling:

> Then he told them many things in parables, saying: "A farmer went out to sow his seed. As he was scattering the seed, some fell along the path, and the birds came and ate it up. Some fell on rocky places, where it did not have much soil. It sprang up quickly, because the soil was shallow. But when the sun came up, the plants were scorched, and they withered because they had no root. Other seed fell among thorns, which grew up and choked the plants. Still other seed fell on good soil, where it produced a crop—a hundred, sixty or thirty times what was sown. He who has ears, let him hear." (Matthew 13:3–9)

In Jesus' explanation of the story, he makes it clear that this story is an analogy for a basic spiritual lesson, in which the seed represents the Word of God. Remember the Reveal study showed that a person's interaction with Scripture was the key influencer in determining spiritual growth, something Jesus affirmed. He went on to explain that the soil represents the condition of the heart. At another point we'll examine the story a bit more in depth, but here we see the basic components of the faith aspect of spiritual formation: seed, soil, and cultivation involving the proper environment for germination and growth. When these elements are in proper alignment, growth is inevitable. Of course, survival depends upon sunlight, water, weather, and a hundred and one other factors. Yet the basic elements of growth for most living things are fairly simple to define.

SOCIAL AND ECONOMIC LIFE AT THE TIME OF CHRIST

At the time of Christ, people understood the process of growing things. Many of the stories Jesus told had to do with agriculture. Not much changed in the technology of agriculture from the time of Christ until John Deere invented the steel plow in the 1830s. That invention was the biggest single innovation in agriculture until this century. Most of the food at the time of Christ was consumed not far from where it was grown, with a few exceptions. Frequently, people ate what they grew, or what they could barter for. They were intimately acquainted with the entire process Jesus described in the parable of the sower, regardless of their economic or social station in life. One did not need to walk far down a Roman road in first century Palestine to see and smell, to experience firsthand, the organic production of agricultural commodities. As we read the Gospels and walk with Jesus and the disciples, we see it all—a virtual historical record of how things grow: barns, vineyards, fields, pastures, gardens, orchards, wells, grain, grapes, olives, figs, fruit, corn, vegetables, sheep, cows, chickens, pigs; the list could go on and on.

AMERICAN CONTRASTS

In contrast, most modern Americans or people in the Western world have very limited acquaintance with the process of how the food they purchase in the grocery store actually made its way to their shopping cart. I remember asking my youngest daughter when she was about three years old if she knew how to milk a cow. "First you go to the refrigerator and get some milk, and then you give it to the cow" was her reply. When I pressed the point about wanting to know where the milk actually came from, "The store" was her immediate and serious answer, based upon her firsthand knowledge. After all, she had been to the grocery store many times and we almost always came home with a gallon or two of milk. Although not as naïve as a three-year-old, many people are virtually clueless about the details of farm life, thus far removed from the stories Jesus told and the lessons he was trying to impart about spiritual growth.

There are presently over 285 million people living in the United States. Of that population, less than 1 percent claim farming as an occupation (and about 2 percent actually live on farms). In contrast, early in the twentieth century, only 28 percent of Americans lived in metropolitan areas, while by 2000 that figure was more than 80 percent.[3] According to the 1900 census, more than one third of Americans lived on farms and there were 10.4 million people (38 percent of the adult workforce) employed in agriculture in the United States, earning an average wage of $20.23 per month.[4]

THE ORGANIC CONNECTION

In our increasingly urbanized environments, stories about farm life and growing things lose much of their potential impact because they seem culturally irrelevant. That is precisely why the growing cadre of organically conscious consumers might foster a new appreciation for the basic components of spiritual formation as Jesus taught and practiced it. Let me randomly list a few of those components, and we'll explore how they fit into the organic spiritual formation process:

- Animal/vegetable/mineral/people/places/things
- Design/planning/purpose/intentionality
- Development/growth/stages of life/seasons
- Earth/soil/heart/water
- Seed/Jesus/Scripture/evangelism
- Wind-air/oxygen/carbon dioxide/life/Holy Spirit
- Fire/sunlight/photosynthesis/chemistry/Holy Spirit
- Journey/exercise/disciplines/worship/stories
- Weather/water/temperature/character development/spiritual vitality
- Taste (salty, bitter, sour, sweet)/personality/gifts/skills
- Pest control/disease/struggles/suffering/fruit/accountability
- Care/nurture/community/teamwork/fellowship/prayer

A LEVEL PLAYING FIELD

As we begin to explore different components of organic spiritual formation, it is helpful to remind ourselves again that becoming a fully developed follower of Jesus Christ does not depend upon social status, cultural setting, level of education, or intellectual capacity. In fact, some of these personality or socioeconomic factors could potentially limit our ability to grow. Perhaps that is why Richard Foster mentions "intentionality" as a basic component of spiritual transformation. Of course, it does take more than good intentions to grow spiritually. Someone has said, "Unless you marry intention to action, you end up with only a brief affair." It requires a marriage of intention with action to produce spiritual growth.

If one feels no need to grow spiritually, it is difficult to generate the intent to do so. That is precisely why the Holy Spirit and the Word of God combine to help us to grow, even when we seem to lack the means. The writer of Hebrews states, "For the word of God is living and powerful, and sharper than any two-edged sword, piercing even to the division of soul and spirit, and of joints and marrow, and is a discerner of the thoughts and intents of the heart" (Hebrews 4:12, NKJV).

Peter reminds us that, "His divine power has given us everything we need for a godly life through our knowledge of him who called us by his own glory and goodness" (2 Peter 1:3). God provides the basic components for spiritual formation, regardless of our station in life. We simply need to cooperate with the process and growth will follow—it's organic.

FOR FURTHER PERSONAL OR GROUP STUDY

- Early in the chapter seed, sunlight, soil, water, air, and nutrients are mentioned as essential to growth along with biblical references. What other Scriptures come to mind about growth?

- The section on identification focuses on seed. Spiritually, how can you identify or differentiate between good seed and bad seed?

- What are some identifying characteristics of a disciple of Jesus?

- What are your thoughts on the definition for "organic spiritual formation" found in this chapter?

- How would you suggest we measure spiritual growth? How do you do so in your own life and walk with Christ?

- Do you have any experience in growing things in soil? What are your thoughts about the parallels in Scripture between spiritual growth and organic farming?

The Parable of the Sower

ccording to Hebrews 11:1, "Faith is the substance of things hoped for, the evidence of things not seen." The whole concept of faith requires belief in something invisible that cannot be proven. If something can be verified with the scientific method, faith is not required. Yet faith is more than just an abstract concept. So how can you describe something you cannot see? How can faith be described in concrete terms? How did Jesus do it? He did it by both showing and telling. The parables of Jesus provided a bridge to help his listeners cross the chasm of doubt and enter the realm of faith.

Parables are stories with a punch. Jesus told at least thirty-nine of them in the Gospels. "Parable" comes from the Greek words *para*, meaning to come alongside, and *ballo*, meaning to throw something down or in place. Parables take abstract concepts and make them more concrete by use of a story. I could say, "Laying brick is a lot more difficult than it looks." That is an abstract statement—true, but dull. It does not paint you a picture. If I told you in detail the story about the time I decided to lay a new brick hearth in our home on a Saturday afternoon, and how the project ended in frustration and disaster on a Sunday morning, you would have a more concrete example.

The parable of the seed or sower was the first of Jesus' parables that he not only told, but also completely explained. This story is one of the most familiar of all the Jesus' parables and the one that most clearly describes the concept of organic spiritual formation, thus it can also serve as a bridge to further exploration of this theme. It is recorded in Matthew (13:1–23), Mark (4:1–20), and Luke (8:4–10). This story could be easily understood by the common people as they were very familiar with the context. Here is the story as Matthew told it:

That same day Jesus went out of the house and sat by the lake. Such large crowds gathered around him that he got into a boat and sat in it, while all the people stood on the shore. Then he told them many things in parables, saying: "A farmer went out to sow his seed. As he was scattering the seed, some fell along the path, and the birds came and ate it up. Some fell on rocky places, where it did not have much soil. It sprang up quickly, because the soil was shallow. But when the sun came up, the plants were scorched, and they withered because they had no root. Other seed fell among thorns, which grew up and choked the plants. Still other seed fell on good soil, where it produced a crop—a hundred, sixty or thirty times what was sown. He who has ears, let him hear."

The disciples came to him and asked, "Why do you speak to the people in parables?" He replied, "The knowledge of the secrets of the kingdom of heaven has been given to you, but not to them. Whoever has will be given more, and he will have an abundance. Whoever does not have, even what he has will be taken from him. This is why I speak to them in parables: Though seeing, they do not see; though hearing, they do not hear or understand. In them is fulfilled the prophecy of Isaiah: 'You will be ever hearing but never understanding; you will be ever seeing but never perceiving. For this people's heart has become calloused; they hardly hear with their ears, and they have closed their eyes. Otherwise they might see with their eyes, hear with their ears, understand with their hearts and turn, and I would heal them.' But blessed are your eyes because they see, and your ears because they hear. For I tell you the truth, many prophets and righteous men longed to see what you see but did not see it, and to hear what you hear but did not hear it. Listen then to what the parable of the sower means: When anyone hears the message about the kingdom and does not understand it, the evil one comes and snatches away what was sown in his heart. This is the seed sown along the path. The one who received the seed that fell on rocky places is the man who hears the word and at once receives it with joy. But since he has no root, he lasts only a short time. When trouble or persecution comes because of the word, he quickly falls away. The one who received the seed that fell among the thorns is the man who hears the word, but the worries of this life and the deceitfulness of wealth choke it, making it unfruitful. But the one who received the seed that fell on good soil is the man who hears the word and understands it. He produces a crop, yielding a hundred, sixty or thirty times what was sown." (Matthew 13:1–23)

This story illustrates the four components of spiritual formation studied in the *Reveal Survey*: exploring Christ, growing in Christ, close to Christ, and Christ-centered.

THE SOWER

Unlike modern gardeners who would use a rototiller to prepare the garden plot and carefully add soil amenities to achieve a good balance of nutrients and pliability, the sower in Jesus' story was definitely low-tech. While we like to plant our crops in straight rows, the sower in Jesus'story took a broadcast approach. He held a bag or vessel filled with seed in the left hand and scattered the seed with a practiced motion with the right hand. The seed was usually scattered on untilled ground. Then with a hoe, plow, or harrow, the ground would be scratched or turned to cover the seed. Thus, the one who "went forth to sow" might not know the subsurface soil condition until he started to work the soil to cover the seed. So what are the other purposes for plowing or breaking up the soil? Actually, there are several:

- Breaking up the soil destroys the present vegetation and gives room for the new plants to grow. It gets rid of the old and makes way for the new. In a spiritual sense, Paul wrote, "Therefore, if anyone is in Christ, he is a new creation; old things have passed away; behold, all things have become new"(2 Corinthians 5:17, NKJV).

- Heavy soils with too much clay need the addition of organic compost material to help make them looser and workable. Breaking up the soil prepares it for the germination of the seed and growth of the new plant. Soft, pliable soil makes it easier to actually plant the seeds in the ground, protects the seed, and makes it easier for the young plants to spread their roots and grow.

- Breaking up the soil makes it easier to pull out weeds and other undesirable plants, which will grow along with the desired crop. In a home garden, it is a lot easier to pull a weed out of softened soil than hardened soil!

- Pliable soil more readily accepts water and nutrients, which may be applied to bring life and nutrition to the growing plants.

By interpretation, the sower in this story is anyone who sows the Gospel. In other words, anyone who is telling others about Jesus in word or deed is a sower. We can sow the seed through the entire orbit of human experience: being, thinking, feeling, and doing. The verb "went" is used to describe the sower's action, his "doing." He "went out to sow." The action verb denotes a conscious decision by the sower to leave his place of security and safety and go with determination and intentionality to sow some seed.

THE SEED

As already mentioned, the seed is the Word of God. We call it the Bible, or Scripture. It is good seed. It can be trusted, and it will accomplish its purpose (see Isaiah 55:11). To be good sowers, however, we should be familiar with the seed and its characteristics so we can sow it wisely. Likewise, seekers must make some contact with the seed, in order to become familiar with what Jesus really said and the contents of the Bible. Amazingly, many people who have never read the Bible think they know what it says. Contact with the seed is a first step in exploring Christ.

THE SOIL

Much depends upon the soil. Human beings are forever tied to the soil, as God created man from "the dust of the earth" (Genesis 2:7). Scientists tell us that our bodies are composed of water combined with the elements of the earth. Although impractical on a large scale, the condition of soil can be changed by adding amenities to make it softer or more pliable, and nutrients can be added to make it more fruitful. Likewise, human beings can change from their naturally hardened and fallen state, through the redemption of Jesus Christ. The best, brightest, and most beautiful among us should remember that we are all basically a bag of dirt, and we will all one day return to the soil.

Farmers and gardeners know that there are four basic soil types: clay, silt, loam and sand. Other conditions in and on the soil determine the success or failure of the crop. In much the same way, Jesus discussed four planting (soil) conditions in this parable.

The first describes seed that fell "by the wayside" (NKJV) or "on the footpath" (NLT). This would indicate a hardened, compacted soil that would be almost impossible to cultivate A clay soil could easily fit this description. Since clay is used to make everything from bricks to pottery, you can see how difficult it would be for seeds to sprout there.

Next, the seeds fell on stony ground The stones might not have been apparent until the sower began to cultivate the soil and realized the ground was filled with rocks. Since much of Israel is very rocky, this must have been a fairly common occurrence. We also know that a human heart can be hard and deceitful, as Jeremiah 17:9 tells us. Just as soil might appear to be good on the surface, but have rocks below or a hardpan under the topsoil, so we can look pretty good on the outside, but have internal problems.

The third description is of seeds that fell "among thorns." Here again, we see something below the surface that wasn't evident to the sower from first glance. The thorns "sprang up" along with the seed. The weed seeds may have been in the soil all along, or the weeds might have been just hacked off at the surface, only to spring back from the roots stronger than ever.

The final description is of seeds that fell on "good ground." The good ground would be a favorable type of pliable soil with the right conditions and nutrients available for a good harvest.

THE SURVIVAL

Only about a fourth of the seed sowed in this parable actually brought forth a harvest. The sower had done his job, but there were mitigating circumstances that determined the eventual outcome and harvest apart from the sowing. Beginning with verse eighteen, Jesus explains what happened to the actual seed sown.

The first seed sowed by the wayside or pathway never had a chance to germinate or even get covered with soil. Luke tells us Jesus described it as being "trodden down." It was destroyed as people walked on it and the remnant was then stolen by the birds.

This seed was a total loss. The description of the pathway is interesting since a lot of people get "walked on" by other people. The application to life is simply that people who hear the Gospel are sometimes very turned off by people who call themselves Christians. For example, Mark David Chapman, the mentally ill individual who assasinated John Lennon in 1980, is a self-professed Christian. He once worked for a Christian organization, attended a Christian college, played in a Christian band and traveled for Christian missions. He told a parole board that if released, he would go from church to church telling his story. I think it is safe to assume that most seekers would be turned off by such an individual, not finding much of Jesus Christ in his actions to emulate, because they shout a message different from his words.

The second description is of seed that fell on stony ground or rocky soil. This seed did germinate (received the word "with joy"!). But it suffered a lack of soil, moisture, and roots. When the sun came out, it got scorched, then withered and died. It remained unfruitful.

The seed on stony ground portrays a person who wants to believe and allows the Word of God to begin to work in his life. Taking baby steps of faith, he may be emotionally charged up, but spiritually unchanged. Thus, he may have moved from "exploring Christ" to beginning growth, but the growth was aborted prematurely. He (or she) never gets really connected to the Lord, and never takes root. When hard times come because of persecution or trouble, the person's faith just withers and dies.

The third bunch of seeds fell among thorns. The seeds germinated, but the thorns or weeds grew up alongside them and they eventually choked out the good seed. Jesus said, "Now he who received seed among the thorns is he who hears the word, and the cares of this world and the deceitfulness of riches choke the word, and he becomes unfruitful" (Matthew 13:22, NKJV).

Many people are slowly being choked to death by the cares and things of this world. That is why our focus should remain heavenward, "looking unto Jesus the author and finisher of our faith" (Hebrews 12:2, NKJV). The more things we have, the more things have us. We become enslaved by the care and maintenance of our possessions. (Jesus told another parable about weeds that we will explore in a future chapter.)

The final picture Jesus portrays is of seed that fell in good soil. It germinated, grew, and brought forth a crop. Jesus said, "But the one who received the seed that fell on good soil is the man who hears the word and understands it. He produces a crop, yielding a hundred, sixty or thirty times what was sown" (Matthew 13:23).

Jesus said a key to producing spiritual fruit is "hearing and understanding" it. We understand Scripture as we are nurtured in Christ. We begin with the basics of the Gospel and go on to learn more about what it means to serve the Lord and follow His Word.

WHAT DOES IT MEAN?

Each person responds to the Gospel differently. Our responsibility is to scatter the seed and help provide the best conditions possible for it to germinate. But we must realize some situations are beyond our control. That is why we must carefully water the seed with our prayers.

Some seed is totally ineffective because Satan snatches it from the hearts of the receivers. Occasionally, the seed falls where it receives an instant but only superficial reception. When difficult circumstances arise, it becomes quickly evident that there is no real commitment. Sometimes the seed begins to take root, only to be suffocated by the cares and concerns of life.

Some seed falls on fertile and receptive ground and produces fruit. Even when the seed is established and grown to maturity, Jesus made it clear that there would be varying results. Some would bring forth a lot of fruit, others a little. Under the ideal circumstances, a person organically grows in the Lord and brings forth fruit, moving through the stages of exploring Christ, growing in Christ, becoming close to Christ, and finally growing to be Christ-centered. The environment makes all the difference. That is why it is important to provide nurturing environments, so that faith, life, and community can develop and sustain spiritual formation and growth.

A SOWER STORY

More than thirty-five years ago, Jodi and I were a newly married couple attending college and living in an apartment complex in Eugene, Oregon. Our next-door neighbors were also recently married and we became good friends. Over time, we shared our faith with John and Kristi.

Although good, moral people with some church background, neither had much exposure to the Gospel prior to our acquaintance. After many conversations about Jesus and the Bible, the seed began to take root in their hearts, and their seed of faith began to grow. John and Kristi developed a vibrant relationship with Jesus that we were privileged to help nourish and cultivate. We have remained in touch through all these years. About two years ago we received this note from Kristi:

I am taking a class and this past week we had to write our life story. It was part of a long exercise of forming our timeline and seeing God's sovereign hand in our life. I have to tell you, you both played a big part in my story and now everyone knows that you two are the ones who shared the Gospel with us and answered all our questions. Have we ever said, "Thank you?" You have had such an impact in our lives and I can not imagine our lives if you were not apart of it. Thank you for your love and prayers all these years, you have been a gift from God. You planted a seed and God has let it sprout and grow.

John and Kristi's influence extends to their children, extended family, neighbors, fellow workers, and countless others they have touched over the years. Through their vibrant faith, lives, and community relationships they have sown seeds that continue to produce fruit.

Remember, it all begins with a seed.

FOR FURTHER PERSONAL OR GROUP STUDY

1. How can faith be described in concrete terms?

2. Why do you think Jesus told stories?

3. What do you take away from Jesus' parable about the seed sower?

4. How is the Bible like seed?

5. How would you describe the soil in your heart? Are there people you know who might illustrate the various types of soil described in this parable?

6. Think of John and Kristi who were mentioned in this chapter. Are there people who planted good seed in your life, and how do you feel about them?

CHAPTER FIVE

Our Stories and Faith

As we already described, Jesus told stories as a basic teaching tool. History has often been described as "his story." Because stories convey emotional energy, narratives do more than tell facts; they evoke feelings and engage the reader in the drama. Not only was Jesus a master storyteller, but the Gospels are a continuing story of his life and ministry.

Jesus' stories or parables involved common, ordinary things that everyday people could relate to. His stories covered topics such as gardening, building, investments, birth, parenting, death, and everything in between. Jewish history was formed from oral tradition, and Jesus was a master at capturing the attention of his listeners through storytelling.

On the farm, stories used to frame much of our conversation. Although I could have quoted my mom and dad's stories about farm life in the good old days word-for-word by the time I was ten, I cannot escape the fact that I learned them by hearing those stories told repeatedly, with emotion and passion. What parent hasn't placed his child against a wall and taken a ruler to mark his height at a particular date? Over time, those marks on the wall tell a story—actually many different stories. Virtually everything on the farm reflects life and has a story to tell. The land itself, with its hills, valleys, streams, forests and fields, tells a story through the years. We often use the expression, "if walls could talk." If they could, then the various homes, barns, and buildings on a farm would house memories that could be told and re-told throughout the generations. Even the equipment and livestock have stories to tell.

Lessons can be learned by the curious and those willing to take the time to listen.

We live in a time of rapid change—you would certainly know that unless you've been living the past decade on a deserted island without media or internet access. So why state the obvious? Perhaps it is because the church is often several years behind the rest of the world in grasping the significance of matters that affect social transformation. For example, many adults in North America could not have imagined living without a telephone in the home—it had become a standard item that signified a family's transition into the modern age. When I was growing up, a family was known by their telephone number as much as anything else. Yet the days of land-line phones are probably numbered as younger generations do not see the need for an antique connected to the wall when they have an iPhone, Android, or tablet device that can do so much more. In fact, the days are probably numbered for cable television as well with so much programming available via the internet and with new open source applications and media enabled wide screen televisions that enable you to watch internet content, not to mention the proliferation of apps for smartphones.

VIRAL

In a word, "viral" describes the rapid evolution of change in our social structure. Like a virus that can be rapidly transmitted from person to person, we now have the technology to incorporate change at an exponential rate. A few years ago, a video made its way across the internet via YouTube featuring a frumpy forty-seven-year-old Scottish woman who made a splash singing on the British version of *American Idol*. Within a week, it had been watched millions of times by people across the world and today Susan Boyle is a star. Applications like Facebook, Twitter, Instagram, and a host of others, make it possible to communicate an idea, concept, or event to hundreds of millions of people in a relatively short period of time.

When I was growing up, the primary source of income on our farm came from raising chickens, about a half million fryers per year. At any given time, we had more than 100,000 chickens to care for. With that number of fowl in one location, the potential for a virus to cause wide-spread destruction was very real. A neighbor about a mile away raised thousands of laying hens, who were also susceptible to the same diseases as our fryers. Whenever the winds blew from that direction, my dad worried that some disease would travel in the wind and infect our birds.

But a virus isn't always a bad thing. The Gospel of Jesus Christ is good news, and it moves in a viral fashion, from person to person. That is the way it happened with Jesus and his disciples, and it is the way it happens today. It is an organic process. A friend tells a friend who tells a friend. And so the Gospel spreads, as with our friends John and Kristi.

A NEW TESTAMENT FAITH STORY

The first chapter of John's Gospel tells a few more details about how Jesus first engaged his disciples. The story begins with John the Baptist making a declaration that Jesus was the "lamb of God" (John 1:36). At that point Andrew, one of John's disciples, followed Jesus and spent the day with him. We can read from the text what happened next:

> The first thing Andrew did was to find his brother, Simon, and tell him, "We have found the Messiah" (which means the Christ). Then Andrew brought Simon to meet Jesus. Looking intently at Simon, Jesus said, "You are Simon, the son of John—but you will be called Cephas" (which means Peter). The next day Jesus decided to go to Galilee. He found Philip and said to him, "Come, be my disciple." Philip was from Bethsaida, Andrew and Peter's hometown. Philip went off to look for Nathanael and told him, "We have found the very person Moses and the prophets wrote about! His name is Jesus, the son of Joseph from Nazareth.""Nazareth!" exclaimed Nathanael. "Can anything good come from there?" "Just come and see for yourself," Philip said. As they approached, Jesus said, "Here comes an honest man—a true son of Israel." "How do you know about me?" Nathanael asked. And Jesus replied, "I could see you under the fig tree before Philip found you." Nathanael replied, "Teacher, you are the Son of God—the King of Israel!" Jesus asked

him, "Do you believe all this just because I told you I had seen you under the fig tree? You will see greater things than this." Then he said, "The truth is, you will all see heaven open and the angels of God going up and down upon the Son of Man." (John 1:41–51, NLT)

I love this story and it illustrates the viral nature of the Gospel of Jesus Christ. Notice the progression here: first John the Baptist told Andrew, then Andrew told his brother Simon. They both had an impact on their friend Philip who also answered Jesus' call. Then Philip told his brother Nathanael about Jesus. The good news about Jesus spread organically, virally, by word of mouth. And the invitation was simple, "Come and see for yourself."

Did you notice how Nathanael was skeptical about Jesus because he was from Nazareth? Nathanael, like many people then and now, harbored prejudices about certain places or people. We can imagine that Nathanael had been influenced by stories he had heard about Nazareth, and his own prejudice made it difficult for him to assume that a place like Nazareth could produce anything extraordinary.

It is easy to see how an encounter with Jesus moved Nathanael from his skeptical position to a place of faith in the Lord. Instead of chastising him, Jesus called him "an honest man, a true son of Israel." No doubt Nathanael was a straight talker, someone who shared his opinions freely. Rather than pointing out his blind spot of prejudice, Jesus commended him for his authenticity.

Many Bible scholars believe that Nathanael was also known as Bartholomew, as perhaps Nathanael was his first name. John only refers to him as Nathanael, while the other three Gospel writers do not mention Nathanael, only Bartholomew. According to various traditions, Bartholomew took the Gospel to India, Ethiopia, and Armenia, among other places. He reportedly died as a martyr by being tied in a sack and thrown into the sea.

When woven together, we see in this series of encounters with Jesus the incredible power of story in producing organic spiritual formation. We also see the compelling power of an invitation, "Come and see." This illustrates the fact that organic spiritual formation also has a viral component. As a person grows and experiences Jesus Christ, those experiences are shared and friends are encouraged to grow in Christ in the process.

In the small church I attended as a child, we regularly had "testimony" times, during which individuals would share something meaningful from their personal journey with Christ over the past week. Even though this sometimes seemed cheesy or predictable, the truth is, I enjoyed hearing most of those stories, and they often did inspire me to spiritual growth. I can attribute much of my early spiritual formation to these conversations. Although using a completely different environment and technology, I am beginning to witness those same "testimony" conversations via the internet through e-mails, blogs, Facebook, and Twitter. One can only imagine the possibilities of spreading the Gospel and principles of spiritual formation through this viral and organic application of new technology.

MY FAITH STORY

Although I was raised in church and loved Jesus from an early age, I had a life-changing encounter with Jesus Christ through the work of the Holy Spirit as a seventeen-year-old high school junior, and I have never been the same since. Even though I was basically a good person and a good student before then, I had drifted away from the early roots of my faith. Perhaps this was due in part to a crisis that took place in our local church when I was a seventh grader that left me somewhat embittered toward the church for a season during my teenage years.

The crisis involved our local congregation voting to remove our pastor. Although he barely made the vote to remain, the circumstances clouded my perspective of Christianity. Admittedly I was young and certainly not privy to all of the details. What I did know, however, troubled me. I knew that Jesus expected his followers to love one another and although I could not find chapter and verse for it, I suspected he did not want a church board or congregation to be divided and try to "fire" a pastor.

Our pastor at the time was young—in his twenties. He brought a breath of fresh air into our church and throngs of new people came to hear his powerful preaching. He and his wife were very musically talented as well. This was back around 1967, and I can still remember him playing the electric guitar and saxophone in our services. I thought it was great! Apparently some of our more dignified members did not.

In time, our congregation actually split. My family stayed, but many people left, including the family of my best friend. And it wasn't long before our pastor left as well. Up to that point, I had been actively involved in church and had felt a call to ministry. I placed all that on the back burner for a number of years, thinking, "If that is how Christians are, I am not sure I really want to be a part of it."

It seems somewhat ironic that I now spend much of my time consulting with churches and working with pastors and boards in conflicted circumstances. Perhaps my own experience as a teenager has helped make me sensitive to the potential fallout and collateral damage that occurs when professed followers of Jesus don't act like they are following Jesus. Conflict is inevitable in life. But it can be managed peacefully, in a way that honors Jesus Christ and protects the innocent. We do well to remember that our actions have an impact on those around us. Many children are perplexed by the disconnect they observe between the professed beliefs and actual behaviors of certain Christian people.

By the time I was seventeen, I was cynical, skeptical, and miserable. I had tried finding contentment and excitement in other places, and was gaining a reputation as more of a party animal than a serious student. Yet deep down I knew that my life had a higher purpose. I also knew that though people had disappointed me, Jesus had never done so. In addition, I could not shake the growing conviction that I was on a slippery slope and needed to fully surrender my life to Jesus Christ. I now believe that this was the Holy Spirit working in my heart in response to the prayers of my family.

As a side note, perhaps you are reading this as one who has become disillusioned with the church, or more specifically people in a specific church. Perhaps you count yourself as a "de-churched" person. May I encourage you to recognize that human beings are not infallible, and disappointment is a sad reality of life. The best advice I ever received was simply, "Keep your eyes on Jesus."

Growing resentment and even cynicism sets in as the default attitude when you focus on the people who hurt you instead of the person of Christ, with tragic results. Resentment is like taking poison and expecting the other person to die—it embitters your soul and chokes the life out of your spirit. Imagine resentment as inviting people you do not like to take up residence in your mind, rent-free, and then giving them control to sabotage your thoughts and emotions at their own convenience. Although I may not have accepted this advice as a teenager, I have since learned that grudges are like hand grenades. They are made to explode, so it is best to get rid of them as soon as possible before they destroy you or those close to you.

Back to my own story: I felt a strong inner sense of conviction for my own sin and growing unbelief. However, at the time I showed no signs of being receptive to the Gospel or promptings of the Holy Spirit outwardly. I repeatedly rejected invitations to attend special Christian youth events and generally enjoyed turning every conversation about spiritual matters into an argument. It seemed I was more suited to becoming an attorney than a minister, and even joined a high school club for prospective lawyers. Although I wasn't a hippie, I did have long hair, and I could relate to those who tuned out the establishment and turned on to a different version of reality. I wrote the following poem that reflects my general attitude and outlook on life those days:

CRY AGAINST THE ESTABLISHMENT

All I am is what I'm not.
All I have is what I've bought.
Wearing my mask as I've been taught.
Can you tell that I am sighing?

I smile at you.
You frown at me.
You're disappointed by what you see.
Can you tell that I am trying?

I tried to play by all your rules.
But the umpires are silly fools.
I think I'll sell the family jewels.
Can you tell that I am crying?

Playing games is hard to bear.
I'm hindered by the mask I wear.
Longing for some fresh true air.
Can you tell that I am dying?

In a word, I was looking for authenticity, and I did not expect to find it in church. I often tried to find excuses not to attend church in those days. When I did, I generally sat in the back row with my friends and seriously avoided showing any emotion or sense that I was interested, particularly during the regular "altar calls" at the end of the service. With the organ quietly playing an old song such as "Softly and Tenderly Jesus is Calling," I would grip the back of the pew in front of me and hold on until it was over. I could then temporarily shake off the peculiar feeling that I really should fully surrender my life to Christ, and instead walk out the door, unchanged and unrepentant.

However, I awoke one Sunday in November of 1971 with the sense of needing to surrender my life completely to the Lord so strong that I determined to do so that particular day, no matter what. So when an invitation was given by our pastor to come forward, I virtually ran down the aisle and raised my hands in surrender to Jesus Christ. My heart and voice poured out in prayers of sorrow and repentance. The Holy Spirit touched my life in a significant way. No longer was I engaged in an intellectual relationship, but an emotional and spiritual connection occurred. As tears ran down my blemished teenaged face, I felt truly cleansed on the inside, like I was born again (John 3:3). Love and joy from the Holy Spirit seemed to bubble out of a heart that had formerly been full of anger, bitterness, and pain. I determined at that moment that I would never again turn away from Jesus, but rather keep my focus on him the rest of my days. I loved Jesus, and he had never seemed more real to me.

My experience was dramatic, and perhaps I needed a dramatic experience to keep me on the straight and narrow path with Jesus. That encounter with Jesus changed me from one who was cynical and skeptical about the things of God to one who was convinced about the power of the Holy Spirit and the ability of Jesus to bring redemption and change to a surrendered life. Just as faith is viral, so is unbelief. I realized that I had previously had enough of religion and religious people to inoculate me against it. So I consider it a miracle that in spite of the fact that I'd been vaccinated against Christianity through the actions of Christian people, Jesus somehow reached through my defenses and infected me with his sweet love.

The "Jesus Movement" was in full swing in those days. I started engaging friends in conversations about Jesus. I had conversations with Jesus in prayer, and I learned how to pray for the leading of the Holy Spirit and how to listen to his voice. I started reading the Bible seriously, and during my junior and senior years read it through several times. I memorized Scriptures such as, "Therefore, laying aside all malice, all deceit, hypocrisy, envy, and all evil speaking, as newborn babes, desire the pure milk of the word, that you may grow thereby, if indeed you have tasted that the Lord is gracious" (1 Peter 2:1–3, NKJV).

My time was now spent joyfully attending a number of home Bible study groups besides being actively involved in my own church youth group. I started playing the guitar, singing, and taking opportunities for leadership. I began speaking or sharing my testimony publicly when the opportunities arose. While still a senior in high school, I was able to enroll in a Bible college in Portland, and made the commute every morning, while finishing my high school requirements in the afternoon. My relationship with Jesus gave me direction. I even found it easier to complete my chores on the farm with Jesus at my side. Through faith, life, and community, I grew.

Reflecting back on those days, it would be easy for me as a fifty-something minister today to long for "the good old days" and think that every person should have a dramatic spiritual experience just like mine. I can understand why there is a warm nostalgic feeling associated with a church building, altar call, specific songs, and a particular style of preaching. All of those things have deep emotional attraction for me. But I dare not confuse those particular methods or artifacts with the essence of the Gospel and the truth of Scripture. People can cross the line of faith in a variety of ways, as long as they are truly coming to Jesus Christ in faith. Every story is unique. And every story is a reflection of the wonderful grace of God through our Lord Jesus Christ.

FOR FURTHER PERSONAL OR GROUP STUDY

1. Why do you think stories are so effective in communicating spiritual truths?

2. How might you weave God's work in your life into the fabric of your story?

3. What emotions describe how you feel about telling your story?

4. Your own faith story can be a powerful thing. You can start by briefly sharing about your life before you came to faith in Christ, then tell how you came to faith in Christ, and then tell how your life has changed since you came to faith in Christ. Writing it out helps; if you have never done so, why not tackle that project this week?

5. If you are part of a small group, share your faith story with the group.

6. Pray about opportunities to share your faith story. Who knows, it might go viral!

A Continuum of Belief

Because faith involves things not seen, another picture might serve as a bridge to help us visualize what it looks like to cross a line of faith and become a believer, or follower of Jesus. This process involves change, and change can be challenging.

While growing up on the farm, I recall the close relationship we enjoyed with one of our neighbors, Mr. Walter Reed, who lived and farmed adjacent to our place. Nearing retirement age, he put his place up for sale, envisioning a life of leisure in town, far away from the daily chores of farm life. Unfortunately, he passed away soon after implementing his plan.

Our new neighbor on the Reed place came from California. Ostensibly, he wanted to be a farmer, although he had no actual experience as such. He entered the arena with optimism, like Oliver Douglas on the old *Green Acres* television show that was popular at the time, leaving behind city life for the simpler life on the farm. He also took on considerable debt to purchase new equipment and upgrade facilities on the old place. It didn't take long for his enthusiasm to wane, however. Life on the farm is not a stroll in the park. Eventually, long hours, hard work, and diminishing profits took their toll. Although he tried his best, the handwriting was on the wall. After a series of similar ownership failures, the old Walter Reed farm today is occupied by a suburban subdivision.

Although a lot of people imagine a simpler life, few have the courage to actually implement their plans. To make such a move involves risk, and the odds of potential failure often outweigh the potential profits. Thus many people choose the security of the known, however painful, over the unknown. Until the pain of staying where you are is greater than the pain of making a change, most people remain stuck where they are.

JESUS, LIFE COACH AND HEALER

Jesus once asked a man, "Do you want to be well?" This particular individual was paralyzed, and had been in that condition for thirty-eight years. Without any hope of a medical solution to his problem, his daily routine was to sit by a pool in the hope that a miracle would take place via the healing waters. Until then, he was dependent upon the charity of others for his sustenance.

So when Jesus asked the question, "Do you want to be well?" one would think he would quickly respond in the affirmative. Instead, he made an excuse. Apparently the years of paralysis had also paralyzed his motivation, hope, and faith. Here is the context of the conversation:

> Now there is in Jerusalem by the Sheep Gate a pool, which is called in Hebrew, Bethesda, having five porches. In these lay a great multitude of sick people, blind, lame, paralyzed, waiting for the moving of the water. For an angel went down at a certain time into the pool and stirred up the water; then whoever stepped in first, after the stirring of the water, was made well of whatever disease he had.
>
> Now a certain man was there who had an infirmity thirty-eight years. When Jesus saw him lying there, and knew that he already had been in that condition a long time, He said to him, "Do you want to be made well?"
>
> The sick man answered Him, "Sir, I have no man to put me into the pool when the water is stirred up; but while I am coming, another steps down before me."
>
> Jesus said to him, "Rise, take up your bed and walk." And immediately the man was made well, took up his bed, and walked. (John 5:2–9a, NKJV)

Did you notice the response of the paralyzed man? Rather than seeing the potential in trusting Jesus to heal him, he indicated that someone else was to blame for his situation. If he only had someone who could help him, someone who would be there for him at the right time—then he, too would be healed. Like so many, this man was looking for human help to fill the needs that only God can fill.

Jesus seemed to ignore his excuse, and simply encouraged him to stand and walk. Following Jesus' command, the man stood and was healed—walking away from that place of interminable despair for the first time in thirty-eight years!

This story is interesting on a couple of levels. First, Jesus engaged this particular man. Jesus loves hopeless people and he longs to have a relationship with them. Second, he listened to him. Even though he did not specifically respond to his excuse as far as we know from the scriptural record, he did listen to him—the man's words are recorded in the Bible. Finally, despite the man's faulty theology or excuses, Jesus was willing to do a work in his life, and he did.

APOLOGETICS AND AUTHENTICITY

Over the years, I have met many people who seemed to have a multitude of objections to placing their faith in Jesus Christ. Too often I used their objections as an opportunity to engage in an argument, hoping to win philosophically, intellectually, or theologically. Believing that I truly cared for their souls, I was determined to convince them that their arguments were full of holes and that placing their faith in God through Jesus Christ makes perfect sense. Sad to say, I did not win many of those arguments.

While I still believe there is a place for apologetics (the branch of theology that is concerned with defending or proving the truth of Scripture), I have come to believe that the best apologetic is both pragmatic and relational. People do not care how much you know if they do not know how much you care. Authentic compassion and love will win over the best argument any day. What if Christians were willing to engage people in the way Jesus was? He generally saved his arguments for the religious people of the day. To the genuine seeker with sincere questions, he responded with grace and kindness. That same approach works well today, after all, how many people do you know who have been won to Christ in an argument?

Our world is full of seekers at different stages in the journey of life. More recently, missional thinkers are moving from the term "seeker" to the term "open," because many people in today's Western world are not actually seeking any spiritual experience or truth, but are open to the idea. However, others are skeptical or even cynical. Some are sincerely seeking truth. Others are skeptical or even cynical. Over time we have learned to place people in easily identifiable boxes. "Just check the appropriate box," we might say if we were to verbalize what we are truly thinking when we encounter someone new.

"Are you a cynic or skeptic? Are you an atheist or an agnostic? Are you a seeker or scoffer? Are you a believer? If so, do you believe just as I do? Would you say you are a Pentecostal or an evangelical? Fundamentalist or liberal? Calvinist or Arminian? Congregational or Episcopal?" In our efforts to clarify things in our own mind, we often muddy the waters of relationship so badly that we cannot see through the turbulence into the needy heart that is truly hurting and seeking relief.

Over the past couple of years I have worked on a diagram that could help us see how people might fit on a continuum of faith, belief, or trust. It can serve as another bridge to connect people from where they are to Jesus. And while this diagram is useful for considering a person's theological location on the journey of faith toward Jesus Christ, it is certainly applicable to many other areas of life. For example, you could choose any particular topic that might be a "hot button" and view it on the continuum. How about organics? I've talked a lot about it in this book thus far. Where do you stand on the topic of organically produced food? Are you a cynic or a skeptic? Do you know the difference between the two? Are you passionately convinced that organic foods represent the key to health and prosperity? Or are you an organic agnostic, admitting you simply do not know?

A CONTINUUM OF BELIEF:

| SUSPICION | | | TENSION | | | TRUST |

Strong Disbelief	Moderate Disbelief	Slight Disbelief	**AGNOSTIC** *"I don't know"*	Slight Belief	Moderate Belief	Strong Belief

UNBELIEVER   ⇐   ⇒   BELIEVER

ORGANIZATIONS/PRODUCTS:
CYNICAL ⇐ SKEPTICAL ⇐ A FEW DOUBTS ⇐ ⇒ PRETTY SURE ⇒ CONVINCED ⇒ CERTAIN

IDEAS:
MYTHS⇐IMPOSSIBLE⇐IMPROBABLE⇐ HYPOTHESIS ⇒ POSSIBLE⇒PROBABLE⇒ABSOLUTES

RELATIONSHIPS:
ADVERSARY ⇐ RESENTMENT ⇐ ANGER ⇐ AMBIVALENCE ⇒ ADMIRATION⇒RESPECT ⇒ ALLY

©2013 Don Detrick

The same strategy for looking at or categorizing religious faith could be applied to a number of other arenas that we are all familiar with. Thus, in trying to move away from sacred and secular delineations, it is sometimes helpful to realize that all people have varying opinions on a wide variety of topics. We all have certain levels of trust or distrust, belief or unbelief in organizations, products, politics, and particularly with people and relationships. It is sometimes helpful to understand and recognize that tension exists between people who have sincerely held beliefs about a variety of topics. Learning to dialogue and have a civil conversation can have better consequences than always arguing and having a war.

The dictionary defines a cynic as a person motivated by selfishness, typically a faultfinder. A cynic is generally more skeptical than a skeptic, who is someone who instinctively or habitually disagrees, doubts, or questions generally accepted conclusions. While a skeptic usually wants more proof, it may be possible to convince a skeptic of a different point of view. A cynic generally doubts everyone's motives, expressing scorn or bitter mockery. Skeptics and cynics both may disregard any level of proof, convinced that it is impossible to actually know anything. In this regard, agnostics may be cynics or skeptics because they typically do not believe it is possible to know for certain if there is a God, heaven, or hell. However, many who would classify themselves as agnostics in today's world would subscribe to a broader definition, simply using the term to convey that they just don't know. That does not mean they are not open to conversation or willing to come to faith at some point.

In very broad terms, we generally accept the notion that there are two types of people in the world, optimists and pessimists. While this is a simplistic conclusion, it is pragmatic for many purposes as most people you meet have a propensity for one or the other dispositions, just as we all tend to be either introverted or extroverted—and there is not necessarily a correlation between optimism and extroversion.

There is an old story about an experiment with two boys, an optimist and a pessimist, that were each placed in a room with nothing but a shovel and a pile of horse manure. When the researchers returned ten minutes later, they found the pessimistic boy crying in the corner, complaining about the stench and begging to be released. But they found the optimistic boy joyfully shoveling the manure and exclaiming, "I just know there has to be a pony around here somewhere!"

The continuum of belief portrayed in the chart is not meant to offer a simplistic way to categorize or label people, but rather a way to envision where people might be on the journey of life. It is specifically useful to consider how we might engage people and help bridge them toward faith in Jesus Christ. And it is particularly helpful to remember that just because a person is at a certain place on the continuum today, he or she may not be taking up permanent residence there. Like the paralyzed man, an encounter with Jesus can help a person to move along toward deeper faith in and closer relationship with Jesus Christ.

FOR FURTHER PERSONAL OR GROUP STUDY

1. Change can be challenging. How quick are you to adapt to change? What is the scariest thing about change for you?

2. Jesus asked a lot of questions. Are you better at asking questions, or giving answers?

3. Which do you prefer, someone telling you what to do, or someone asking you what you need? Why?

4. Look back at the diagram, "A Continuum of Belief." How might you use it in talking to someone about faith in Jesus Christ?

5. Read Hebrews 11:6 again. What are some indications a person is starting to believe?

6. How important are prayer and the work of the Holy Spirit in leading a person toward faith in Jesus?

PART THREE

LIFE

CHAPTER SIX

Homegrown Is Better

Life begins at home. Anyone who has ever raised a garden knows that homegrown produce looks much different from that purchased in a typical grocery supermarket. It even smells different. If you compare a ripe, homegrown tomato with one of those plastic-looking objects from the typical grocery produce department, you know what I mean. The homegrown variety is bright, deep red in color, soft in texture, and smells rich and savory. The store-bought tomato typically looks pale pink, with splotches of green. It feels firm, like a piece of wax. Smell it—it doesn't have any aroma at all. Take a bite of each and there is no comparison. While both resemble a tomato, the homegrown, organic item looks, feels, and smells alive. The one purchased from the grocery store has the appearance and feel of an embalmed facsimile of the real thing. It's no wonder most grocery stores are now selling hothouse-grown "tomatoes on the vine," which may or may not be organically produced but closely resemble the homegrown variety.

My own spiritual journey began as a child at home on the farm. There was never a time I didn't know about Jesus and his love for me. Prayer, and attending Sunday school, church, vacation Bible school, and a myriad of church meetings with my mother were part of my everyday existence and shaped the genesis of my memories. Speaking of memory, the practice of weekly "memory verses" from the Bible via rote repetition formed the backbone of my spiritual formation before I could read a sentence on the printed page. The fact I can quote most of them fifty years later are a testimony to both the enduring quality of God's Word and the efficacy of teaching Scripture to children when they are young.

I realize my story is increasingly unique as the majority of North Americans have not had the kind of home environment that fosters faith or spiritual formation. Most have had no real exposure to the Bible or Jesus, and thus no real context for defining the word "Christian" outside of caricatures gleaned from the media. However, regardless of personal background, anyone can begin a journey of faith from any point. The Gospel is good news for all people at all places and at all times. God has and will provide everything a person needs to grow if only he or she will make the decision to follow Christ.

FIRST STEPS

Just as each human infant must learn to roll over, sit up, crawl, and take first steps, so the path of spiritual formation involves a process. And that process can be as individual as the DNA of the person on the journey of faith. Some children walk before they are eight months old, others may wait until eighteen months or more. Some never crawl, but scoot or roll around, to the delight of their parents. Many falls, bruises, and scrapes come with the journey toward walking and eventually running. No child learns to walk exactly the same way as another, in spite of identifiable milestones along the way.

PAUL'S INSTRUCTIONS

The Apostle Paul presents a dramatic case for the steps to faith in Jesus Christ as he writes to the Roman believers. By the time he gets to Romans chapter ten, though writing primarily to Gentiles, he is making a point of the futility of trying to keep God's law on our own, while Christ has provided the means for forgiveness or justification by paying the penalty for our sins on the cross. He makes a strong case for exercising faith—what we would call today, "crossing the line of faith." While we have tended to formalize and even institutionalize the practice in the twentieth century through altar calls or repeating the "sinner's prayer," the fact remains that repentance and coming to faith in Christ involves a process of both believing and confession. As Paul writes:

For Christ is the end of the law for righteousness to everyone who believes. For Moses writes about the righteousness
which is of the law, "The man who does those things shall live
by them." But the righteousness of faith speaks in this way, "Do
not say in your heart, 'Who will ascend into heaven?'" (that is, to
bring Christ down from above) or, "'Who will descend into the
abyss?'" (that is, to bring Christ up from the dead). But what does
it say? "The word is near you, in your mouth and in your heart"
(that is, the word of faith which we preach): that if you confess
with your mouth the Lord Jesus and believe in your heart that
God has raised Him from the dead, you will be saved. For with
the heart one believes unto righteousness, and with the mouth
confession is made unto salvation. For the Scripture says, "Whoever believes on Him will not be put to shame." For there is no
distinction between Jew and Greek, for the same Lord over all is
rich to all who call upon Him. For "whoever calls on the name of
the Lord shall be saved." (Romans 10:4–13, NLT)

Paul draws a contrast between trying to keep the law and faith in
Jesus Christ and he concludes that "Christ is the end of the law." This
promise is, "to everyone who believes." And where do we get the faith to
believe? Paul says there is no need for us to change our geographic location, no need to ascend to heaven or descend into hell. It is "near you," as
close as your heart and mouth. Salvation comes by believing in our heart
and confessing Jesus Christ with our mouth. And it doesn't matter where
we live, our age, gender, or ethnicity. Wherever we are and whoever we
are, if we "call on the name of the Lord," we will be saved. These are the
first steps of faith, and they begin at home.

HOW DID JESUS DO IT?

Organic spiritual formation tends to flourish in nurturing, familiar
environments. Jesus did not recruit disciples from Rome, Egypt, or Ara-
bia. He selected twelve individuals whom he found in close geographical
proximity to where he grew up, whose language and culture were similar

to his own. God's mission is to all people of every language and culture. But once a person becomes a follower of Christ and takes on the life of a disciple, the initial stages of growth seem to work best in a familiar setting.

HOW COULD WE DO IT?

In a broader sense, this principle can be applied to organic spiritual formation in a local church setting. How often do pastors or church leaders attend conferences where they hear exciting stories about how certain models or styles of "doing church" are enjoying great success? The temptation is to import the same mechanism into their local church setting, a process that is generally met with resistance and ultimately, mediocre results, if not outright failure. This is because one of the most basic principles of organic discipleship lies in the belief that the ever-creative Holy Spirit wants to work in unique ways in different environments, locations, and settings. What works well in one culture or community may not have any impact in another. We may actually hinder the work of spiritual formation by continually looking for ideas from other sources, when the answer may be a homegrown solution hidden closer to where we live. After all, if we believe the answer lies somewhere else, in a different geographical context, we will make excuses for not having made progress. But if we really believe that God has provided everything we need for life and godliness (see 2 Peter 1:3) right where we live, we will start growing at home. Home provides the best nurturing environment for organic spiritual formation.

Of course when I mention "home," it includes a broader context than just the dwelling where you reside. My primary memories of learning the really important lessons in life, from how to feed and dress myself to tying my shoes or riding a bicycle, are all centered in home. But along the way, I learned in more formal, institutional settings. I didn't attend kindergarten, but I have vivid memories of the elementary school I attended for six years and each of the teachers who imprinted my young life and mind. Even earlier, I remember attending Sunday school and church on a weekly basis, and recall the stories, songs, and crafts from those experiences as well as the faces of the teachers, all volunteers for the most part.

They helped me understand that Jesus loves me and has a purpose and plan for my life. They taught me that heaven is a real place, and that I could make a difference on earth by following Jesus and his purposes. These were not foreign concepts to me; they simply reinforced what I was already learning in my home from my parents and siblings.

At one point in my childhood when I was four or five, I came down with rheumatic fever. The condition necessitated inactivity, and for six months or more I was confined to bed under a doctor's care. My Sunday school teacher at the time, Ruth Tilden, made house calls during that period of my young life. I vividly recall her bringing the Sunday school lesson to our home, and she brought her two sons Harold and Leslie with her. It was a welcome relief, in my socially deprived circumstances. I still remember the kindness she showed as she taught, repeating on a weekday in our home what she had taught at church on the Sunday before. God does not require special buildings or programs to provide the means for spiritual growth. Fifty years later, the lessons Ruth taught me still remain a foundational part of the framework for my faith.

AN EXAMPLE FROM THE GOSPELS

In one of the most dramatic moments recorded in the Gospels, Jesus delivered a man from demons. The man was so tormented that he lived naked in a cemetery—a place no respectable Jewish person would visit because of Old Testament ceremonial prohibitions about coming near dead bodies—and Jesus cast a legion of demons out of him, sending them into a herd of pigs (which a good Jewish person would also avoid). The pigs promptly ran off a cliff and died in the sea below.

As you might imagine, this caused a bit of a stir among the people. Curious onlookers from the nearby town approached to see what was happening. Expecting to see the crazy naked man who lived near the tombs, instead they were met with a different scene. Luke records what took place next:

> When those tending the pigs saw what had happened, they ran off and reported this in the town and countryside, and

the people went out to see what had happened. When they came to Jesus, they found the man from whom the demons had gone out, sitting at Jesus' feet, dressed and in his right mind; and they were afraid. Those who had seen it told the people how the demon-possessed man had been cured. Then all the people of the region of the Gerasenes asked Jesus to leave them, because they were overcome with fear. So he got into the boat and left. The man from whom the demons had gone out begged to go with him, but Jesus sent him away, saying, "Return home and tell how much God has done for you." So the man went away and told all over town how much Jesus had done for him. (Luke 8:34–39)

While a lot of observations can be made from the above story, three come to mind. First, Jesus can change lives regardless of the circumstances and setting. No doubt this man's family had virtually given up on him. Certainly no respectable and law-abiding Jewish person would live under such conditions. Yet there is no place and no person out of the reach of God's love and compassion.

Second, I notice that the response of most people to this great miracle was fear, rather than reverence or joy. People often fear what they don't understand. That can be especially true when a friend or family member makes a decision to follow Jesus Christ. Our natural tendency is to avoid or separate from those who are different; that reflects our human nature. Jesus came to counteract this tendency toward division and to reestablish relationship between God and man and improve relationships between our fellow men.

Third, the natural response for the delivered man was to want to stay close to Jesus and his friends—to move on to a safe environment, to get away from the setting that was filled with memories of despair. Of course there may be times when a change of scenery and friends is an important component of breaking old habits or lifestyles. However in this case, Jesus made it clear: "Return home and tell how much God has done for you."

WHY HOMEGROWN IS BETTER

Home is the best environment to grow and spread our faith, maybe because those who know us best provide the perfect laboratory and motivation for spiritual formation. If faith works at home, where we are often at our worst—displaying our authentic selves and expressing our true feelings and actions—it can work in any environment. Perhaps this is because home is also the place where we have the potential to do our best work, the place where we can do the most good, to make the biggest difference in life.

Leadership is best described as influence. Home is where influence grows best. Even though I only spent the first eighteen years of my life there, my life as an adult is a reflection of the influence of persons, places, and things during those formative years of my life. It is during those early years that a parent's influence is greatest. During the teenage years influence is transferred to peers and others as the adolescent turns into an adult and learns to become an individual. Although it may be latent, at some point every adult looks in the mirror and sighs, "I look and act just like my mother (or father)!"

"Watch me!" I often hear my six-year-old granddaughter shout. I cannot tell you how many times I spoke the same phrase to my parents as a child, yearning for their full and undivided attention, hoping they would notice some accomplishment or a job well done. Thankfully, I have good memories of my parents actually listening to me and affirming me. It feels good to be noticed when doing something right. Unfortunately, some children receive only raised eyebrows and raised voices indicating disapproval and a standard that can never be met. Children of all ages need affirmation, as it provides a nurturing environment for growth, whether someone is one or one hundred years old.

If you have children or grandchildren, pay attention to what they are saying and doing. Listen. You will hear them saying, "Watch me! Pay attention to me. I need you to protect me, guide me, and help me to know that I am capable of doing great things in this world. I don't want to be a loser. You'll be there for me, won't you?" Their pleas to you and me are a reflection of the human condition, as every human heart longs for God's watchful protection, care and approval—a safe place to call "home."

GEOGRAPHY AND HORTICULTURE

When it comes to cultivating plants for food, geography is perhaps the most significant determiner of what to grow. You don't expect to grow coconuts in Alaska or coffee in Scandinavia. Each area of our pale blue dot (as the late astronomer Carl Sagan called planet earth) has plant species that are indigenous and others that, though imported, thrive in that specific geographical zone.

Of course I am most familiar with the small parcel of land in Oregon known as the Chehalem Valley, where I grew up. Our farm bordered the banks of Chehalem Creek and the valley and surrounding hillsides were a fertile microcosm of Oregon's Willamette Valley. During my growing up years, the predominant crops included berries of every kind. (Newberg was home to the annual Berry Festival.) I spent my childhood picking strawberries every summer to earn money for school clothes. Green beans and other vegetable crops flourished as did the orchards on nearby hillsides that grew abundant crops of plums, walnuts, and hazelnuts (filberts). I attended Dundee Elementary School, and the small community of Dundee was known at the time as "The Nut Capital of the World" (undoubtedly a slogan with a variety of interpretations!).

However, it is important to note that the crops cultivated by one generation do not always have the same appeal to future generations. This has to do with market conditions, consumer preferences, cultivation techniques, harvest technology, and many other factors. Before my time, in the late nineteenth century and early twentieth century, Newberg was known as a center of the dairy industry. In fact, our family farm was a dairy before I was born. And today the large structures in our area that we used to dry prunes and nuts are crumbling relics of the past.

The Chehalem Valley and the surrounding verdant hillsides are now known as the center of Oregon's thriving wine country, with Dundee serving as the home to many wineries. I find that somewhat ironic as the communities of Newberg and Dundee were "dry" towns during most of my growing up years—strongly influenced by the Quakers and many evangelical churches in the area. My point is simply to note that the same soil and conditions can in fact produce different crops, and even different cultures. The wine-tasting crowds thronging to Dundee these days are definitely more socially upscale than the folks that used to come there for the nuts back in the day when I was a boy!

Because I am a lifelong resident of North America, I am familiar with agricultural methods and crops on my continent. For purposes of illustration, most North American gardeners are familiar with maps out-lining various climate zones in the United States and Canada. These are found in virtually every book or internet site about gardening. Within these color-coded zones are keys to plants that thrive within the region. If you want a successful garden, you plant seeds that are known to grow and bear fruit in your particular part of the world. The same principle applies regardless of where you reside.

The spiritual parallels may not be quite as obvious. God created the universe with living things and provided the mechanisms and means for reproduction. In the plant world, seeds naturally fall or are blown within close proximity to the parent plant. In other words, if conditions were good for the parent to grow and reproduce in a particular geographical zone, the same will be true for the offspring.

Believe it or not, I like okra, a vegetable of suspicious character to many. Those who recognize it often think of it only as a slimy ingredi-ent in gumbo. I prefer to consume it deep-fried after rolling it in corn meal—a distinctive technique popular in the American southland. I once thought I'd try growing okra in my garden in Oregon. I reasoned that I could lengthen the growing season in Oregon's Willamette Valley by planting the okra seeds early in seed beds under artificial conditions, and later transplant the seedlings into my garden outdoors. While the plants grew spectacularly, there was no fruit. You can successfully grow okra in Oklahoma, but not in Oregon. The location makes all the difference.

During my experiment in growing okra, I knew what I wanted to see as the end product. Despite my vision and good intentions, I never saw my vision fulfilled. Okra simply will not bear fruit in Oregon. It is not sustainable. And that is not a problem for most residents of the state who prefer Oregon's more traditional fruits and vegetables. "Why would I want to raise okra anyway?" most would say. "Who cares?"

Most people don't have an interest in following Christ for the same reasons most do not have any interest in growing okra. The idea seems irrelevant at best and revolting at worst. I suspect that the one reason these perceptions exist has to do with the association between Jesus and his followers.

"What do you think about Jesus?" my wife asked her seatmate on the plane recently. "Oh, I like him, I just don't know about church and all that stuff" she answered. I was sitting on the other side of my wife, and because of my location I was more of a listener than participant in the conversation. Jodi spent the next couple of hours talking to her seatmate and discovered that a bad experience with church and Christians early in life had strongly influenced this woman's adult perceptions about Christianity and the church. By exchanging e-mail addresses, Jodi has continued the conversation with her, pointing her toward Jesus. We have met countless others with similar stories.

Perception is reality for most people, and for many in North America, followers of Jesus are perceived negatively, as evidenced by books on this subject, such as *They Like Jesus but Not the Church*. Certainly the media has played a role in forming people's perceptions of Christians. We are often portrayed as "anti" everything: anti-abortion, anti-equal rights, anti-environment, etc. While these portrayals are biased and generally inaccurate, wouldn't it be wonderful if people did not think Christians were angry hate-mongers? How can we change the inaccurate perceptions?

WHOM SHOULD WE LOOK LIKE?

Within the church we tend to hold a certain image of a mature follower of Christ. This person should act, look, even dress like us. Our vocabularies and tastes in music and perhaps even food for the ubiquitous church potluck should be similar. We reason that the trappings of Christianity that made us grow into a particular variety of believer should automatically produce the same results in others. We wrongly assume that

Sunday school lessons, hymns, sermons, buildings, and meetings became the primary and perhaps only means of grace leading to spiritual growth. We sincerely believe that if we simply replicate the conditions, we will get the same results. Then we face disappointment when replication does not occur or when the growth seems stagnated or unsustainable.

We fail to recognize that the same hometown can produce different-looking fruit and even develop a different culture at different times, as illustrated earlier by my own hometown of Newberg, Oregon. A scientific laboratory can create a clone, but a real living environment produces diversity.

What if we had a vision for developing people who look like Jesus, instead of us? Would that make any difference? Maybe we need to take another look at Jesus. He didn't dress like us, look like us, talk like us, or value the things we typically value. We are sure of those things, although there is no real physical description of Jesus in the New Testament. He had few possessions and reserved his harshest judgments for those who were more religious than relational. So perhaps that is the point we are missing. Jesus didn't enter this world dressed in the twentieth-century trappings of a North American Christian. He didn't hold mass crusades or start a megachurch. In fact he didn't even attend worship services on Sunday. He was a hometown, homegrown boy—made in his Father's image and doing his Father's business within his own unique cultural milieu.

Not long ago Jodi and I attended a church located in the Pacific Northwest whose members hailed from another part of the world. This particular ethnic group is held together in their new home by the roots of their faith. We arrived early, in time for Sunday school. As the activities began I immediately was unexpectedly translated back in my mind to my own upbringing in Oregon. The "opening exercises" complete with singing familiar choruses, calling forth people to celebrate their birthdays and reciting a familiar memory verse were all straight out of our North American evangelical church culture of the 1950s. It was like attending church in a time warp. As the service continued, more familiar elements came into play. "Just like we used to do it," I thought.

Why would a church service for an ethnic group from another part of the world seem so unlike what I know of their own cultural distinctives? It is because they have assimilated and acculturated the same methodology used by the first North American missionaries who came to their land in the 1950s. They still were doing church the way they had been taught by the American missionaries more than a half century earlier. While the church in North America has certainly changed, these dear souls are caught in a mindset that believes the way they originally practiced their faith—church service style—is the best and perhaps only way. It is no wonder that many of their younger generation are leaving for more contemporary worship experiences in their new country, much to the disappointment of their parents.

THE HOLY SPIRIT BRINGS JESUS CLOSE TO HOME

Spiritual formation occurs organically when faith takes root and grows in native soil. The expressions of faith may look different, sound different, or taste different, depending upon the location. Is it too difficult to believe that the Holy Spirit wants to reach people right where they are, using other people who speak in a language they can understand? Isn't that what the Holy Spirit did at Pentecost when the Spirit presented the Gospel to people from diverse languages and cultures in a way they could all understand? And then didn't they take the Gospel back to those who shared similar language and culture, presenting Jesus in a way that could be understood within their own context?

Homegrown Christianity allows Jesus to develop followers through the work of the Spirit. We do best to partner with that work and celebrate the unique flavor and creativity of God in that culture. When I visit Shanghai, Paris, or Tijuana I expect to find different cultures and cuisines than I will find in Akron, Ohio. I also expect that the Christ-followers in each of those locations will look, speak, dress, and act differently. What we have in common is a shared faith in Jesus and hope of eternal life through his redeeming grace. Homegrown faith in Jesus will reproduce itself within its own context, organically.

JESUS IN YOUR HOMETOWN

For the past several years my wife Jodi has written a faith and values column for *The Seattle Times*. Our area is one of the most culturally and ethnically diverse in the nation. We are known for Starbucks, Boeing, Amazon, and Microsoft, not for a strong commitment to the Christian faith or organized religion.

Jodi's mission is simple: to present Jesus to this culturally diverse audience of millions of prospective readers. She does so by presenting stories, often about local people or friends who are making a difference for Jesus. Jodi is careful not to use the Bible as a weapon to beat people over the head with, but she does intentionally weave biblical truths and Scripture into her stories. (You can read dozens of them online by going to www.seattletimes.com and then doing a search for "Jodi Detrick.")

The results are pretty amazing. A woman who had lost a daughter in a tragic airplane crash wrote how a particular column gave her hope. A former university president wrote how he shared a column with a friend. People have written about how they have discovered hope in desperate circumstances, peace in stormy seasons, healing for hurting hearts, and faith in the midst of doubt.

Of course there are always those who react to her columns with incredulity. They cannot believe that a Pulitizer-prize-winning newspaper would publish fables and religious myths, and some are downright venomous in their remarks. But they are all on a journey in the continuum of belief, and it started by reading a column in their hometown newspaper.

FOR FURTHER PERSONAL OR GROUP STUDY

1. "The Gospel is good news for all people at all places and at all times." Why do you think many people don't think of Christianity as "good news"? How could you, your church, family, or small group change that perspective?

2. Read Romans 10:9–13. What do you think it means to "call on the name of the Lord?" Is anything else necessary for a person to come to faith in Christ?

3. What steps should follow the first steps of faith?

4. Think about how we nurture children in growth toward maturity. What parts of that process might apply to new believers in their organic spiritual formation?

5. "Organic spiritual formation tends to flourish in nurturing, familiar environments." Do you agree or disagree? What might be some helps or some hindrances toward spiritual growth in your own home or neighborhood?

6. If someone met Jesus in your hometown, what would he look like?

7. How does our own culture affect our view of Jesus or the church? How does your answer to question #1 above fit into the picture?

CHAPTER SEVEN

Good Nutrition Fuels Growth

My Grandma Detrick lived with us during most of my growing up years. This came about because one morning in the early 1960s my mother called Grandma to check up on her. This was a daily routine. On that particular day, Grandma did not answer the phone. Knowing something was wrong, my parents hurried to Grandma's house about two miles away in town, where they found her on the floor, barely able to move or speak.

Grandma was born in 1877, and by then she was in her eighties. We really didn't expect her to live long, and neither did our family physician. As it turned out, she had no broken bones, but he diagnosed her as malnourished and dehydrated. Living alone, she had simply stopped eating a healthy diet and was virtually skin and bone. The irony in the story is the fact that Grandma's cupboards were full to the brim with home-canned produce of every description. Her well-stocked refrigerator and freezer gave no indication that she did not have enough to eat.

The family met, and though it was suggested by some that Grandma be placed in a nursing home, the eventual decision was for her to move into our home. My dad was the closest child and felt a keen responsibility to follow the biblical injunction to honor his aged parent.

After the move, rather than quickly dying as the doctor predicted, Grandma began to perk up in the social atmosphere of our busy family. My mother lovingly prepared three hearty and nutritious meals for her every day, and she soon regained her health and resumed her regular activities of sewing, visiting friends, crocheting, and church life. She lived for more than ten years, going to be with the Lord in 1974 at the age of 96. Good nutrition added another decade to her life.

NUTRITION: NOW AND THEN

We have more information about nutrition today than any other time in history. Somewhat ironically, in spite of our information overload on the subject—current medical research, health websites, Dr. Oz, warning labels, and infomercials—many of us fail to embrace healthy diet or exercise choices. Unlike people of past generations, our problems in Western society have more to do with an abundance of food to eat rather than a lack of nutrition. Americans who are thirty or more pounds over a healthy weight cost the country an estimated $147 billion in weight-related medical bills in 2008, double the amount a decade ago, according to a study by government scientists and the nonprofit research group RTI International.[1]

Too many choices, temptations, and ultimately too many poor decisions based on uncontrolled appetites rather than hunger contribute to an unhealthy lifestyle. Thus, more and more people who want to pursue healthier food choices are opting for organic nutrition.

At the time of Christ, few people were overweight and everyone ate organic foods. There was nothing else available. Only the wealthy could afford to be "nutritionally enhanced." Most others wondered where they would find their next meal. In his Sermon on the Mount, it is not surprising to hear Jesus teach his followers to pray, "Give us this day our daily bread" (Matthew 6:11, NKJV). Few North Americans today would feel much emotion when they enter this plea. But daily bread was not to be taken for granted by Jesus' audience, and an appeal for divine provision represented a conscious act of faith, trusting God for nutrition that may have been humanly impossible to obtain otherwise.

BREAD

The aroma of freshly baked bread fills the senses with anticipation; few can resist the allure. The smell of baking bread is familiar to people in nearly every part of the world, and it whets the appetite. In biblical times, bread was commonly fashioned from flour made by grinding barley or wheat. Like today, the flour was mixed with water, oil, and yeast or other ingredients to form dough which was baked over a fire or in a clay oven. The bread might be leavened with yeast or remain unleavened, depending both upon the raw materials available and the season of the year. For the most part, the Jewish people at the time of Christ used the sourdough method of bread-making. Each batch of bread was genetically linked to the first batch as they used a small piece of starter dough in the new batch of dough to add the yeast. Then a little bit of the new batch of dough was set aside as starter for the next batch.

Most people at the time of Christ ate a simple diet of available produce. Bread, olives, cheese, butter, yogurt, fruit, nuts, and vegetables formed the staples of diet for the common family, along with water, milk, olive oil, juice, or wine. Meat was eaten on rare occasions, depending upon the family's or individual's economic status. Variety and spices were also limited by geography and financial circumstances. To our palates, the diet would seem rather bland indeed.

Bread was so common that it became a synonym for life itself. Because whole grain could be easily dried and stored, it was grown wherever possible and used as the most basic of foods. When traveling or in a hurry, grain could easily be parched and eaten. At other times, it was eaten raw. Ground into flour and made into bread, it became the primary staple food. Rather than using a knife to slice it as we would commonly do, bread in ancient times was typically "broken" or torn apart. Thus, having a meal was called, "breaking bread."

When Jesus said, "I am the bread of life" in John 6:35, he was making a profound statement to his listeners, who associated bread with life itself. He had just fed a multitude of people and like today, people were anxious to get in line for more of the free bread. He was not speaking of physical bread, however, but spiritual life. Jesus is as necessary for spiritual formation as bread is for physical life.

Later, Jesus used the bread of the Passover to illustrate how his own physical body was about to be broken for the sins of the world. When we eat the bread of communion (or eucharist), we remember that Last

Supper, and that Jesus came in the flesh to become the bread of life for us. He suffered death in his sinless body to purchase salvation for our sinful souls. Every time we come together for communion, we remember the incarnation of Christ and we express appreciation for his sacrificial gift.

In a broader sense, the church is known as "the body of Christ," noting that we who are the "called-out ones" or *ecclesia*, are the physical representation of Jesus Christ on the earth. We are to live incarnational lives and in a figurative sense, be the "bread of life" to those we touch along the way.

NUTRITION, FOOD PRESERVATION, AND INFLUENCE

In New Testament times, food was often consumed shortly after it was produced. With a few notable exceptions, diets were governed by whatever foods were available at the time. Modern food preservation techniques such as freezing, refrigeration, canning, dehydration, or shrink-wrapping were unknown in those days. The only two common preservation methods in use involved drying and/or salting foods.

Dried foods included grains, fish, nuts, dates, raisins, figs, and other fruit. With the dry climate and abundant sunshine in Palestine, drying was one of the simplest and most available means of preserving foods. Dried foods could be consumed at other times of the year, making the season effectively stretch far beyond the time of harvest.

Salt was in abundant supply in Palestine, which had large salt deposits near the Dead Sea. Salt was used to dry and prepare fish for export in Magdala, home of Mary Magdalene. Not only was salt used as a preservative and for seasoning, its healing properties made it one of the few medical treatments readily available for common people. Because it was both common and valuable, salt was used in offerings prescribed by the Old Testament law (see, for example, Leviticus 2:13).

In his Sermon on the Mount Jesus said, "You are the salt of the earth. But if the salt loses its saltiness, how can it be made salty again? It is no longer good for anything, except to be thrown out and trampled by men" (Matthew 5:13).

Jesus used salt as a metaphor for his followers, and even today people use the phrase, "salt of the earth" to describe people who are gracious and kind. In a word, Jesus is taking about influence. As we draw close to Jesus, he influences us, and we in turn influence others. Further drawing upon the metaphor, we can expect to influence others by serving as a preservative, for seasoning, and for healing. I love an old poem by R.L. Sharpe titled, *A Bag of Tools* that expresses the power of influence:

> Isn't it strange how princes and kings,
> and clowns that caper in sawdust rings,
> and common people, like you and me,
> are builders for eternity?
> Each is given a list of rules;
> a shapeless mass; a bag of tools.
> And each must fashion, ere life is flown,
> A stumbling block, or a Stepping-Stone.[2]

TASTE

Our tastes are typically as sophisticated as our economy and geography will allow. Human tongues can distinguish four distinct tastes: sweet, sour, bitter, and salty. It is this combination of tastes that enhance our palate, provide flavor, and make foods interesting. A balanced nutritional diet often consists of foods with a variety of tastes, flavors and textures. (And while I think chocolate designates the very best food group, I recognize that it is possible to have too much of a good thing.)

Our tastes for certain things have to be developed. This is particularly true when we are exposed to particular ethnic foods for the first time. Curry was never an ingredient in my mother's meat and potatoes daily menu repertoire. When I first experienced Indian or Thai foods rich in curry, I can't say I was enthused. Over time and exposure, however, I have not only grown to accept, but to enjoy foods prepared with this spicy ingredient.

We commonly attribute experiences of life to our own personal tastes. Some days we have the sweet experience of feeling loved and accepted. Music and laughter fill our hearts with joy. At other times we experience the bitterness of pain when we feel rejected or betrayed by those we trusted and loved. We have all experienced a sour feeling when sick to our stomach because of worry or grief. Likewise we have all experienced the sting of salty words applied to our wounded hearts.

Sometimes the emotions are so strong and painful we can taste them—and the taste is not good. The Lord can help us to digest each of these strong feelings, the pain of brokenness and hurt feelings, the tragic and traumatic experiences of life. And in the end, he can turn those awful tastes into nutrition that feeds our soul with strength and endurance, and in so doing build our faith.

Psalm 34:8 says, "Taste and see that the Lord is good. Oh, the joys of those who trust in him!" (NLT). In Psalm 119:103 the psalmist exclaims, "How sweet are your words to my taste, sweeter than honey to my mouth!" Those of us who know Jesus have experienced that he is good and that his Word provides sweet nourishment for our souls.

The challenge for those of us who follow Jesus lies in our own ability to be good and sweet. With few exceptions, we lack these attributes naturally. So we grow sweeter and better as we grow more like Jesus. That is the goal of spiritual formation for the follower of Jesus. And when we are sweet and good, it is easier for people who don't know Christ to see the Jesus in us. True missional living, engaging in the mission of God to change our world for Jesus Christ, requires us to offer the bread of life (Jesus) to hungry people we meet.

A NUTRITIONAL MISSIONAL MIRACLE

It was in that very context of human need, hunger, and suffering that Jesus performed one of his greatest miracles, the feeding of the five thousand. The text in chapter six of the Gospel of John describes how Jesus used a young boy's sacrificial gifts of a few fish and pieces of bread to feed a multitude of people.

> Some time after this, Jesus crossed to the far shore of the Sea of Galilee (that is, the Sea of Tiberias), and a great crowd of people followed him because they saw the miraculous signs he had performed on the sick. Then Jesus went up on a mountainside and sat down with his disciples. The Jewish Passover Feast was near.

When Jesus looked up and saw a great crowd coming toward him, he said to Philip, "Where shall we buy bread for these people to eat?" He asked this only to test him, for he already had in mind what he was going to do.

Philip answered him, "Eight months' wages would not buy enough bread for each one to have a bite!"

Another of his disciples, Andrew, Simon Peter's brother, spoke up, "Here is a boy with five small barley loaves and two small fish, but how far will they go among so many?"

Jesus said, "Have the people sit down." There was plenty of grass in that place, and the men sat down, about five thousand of them. Jesus then took the loaves, gave thanks, and distributed to those who were seated as much as they wanted. He did the same with the fish. When they had all had enough to eat, he said to his disciples, "Gather the pieces that are left over. Let nothing be wasted." So they gathered them and filled twelve baskets with the pieces of the five barley loaves left over by those who had eaten. (John 6:1–13)

Here we see Jesus and His disciples confronted with a problem. A large crowd had come to hear Jesus speak. Some Bible commentators infer that the crowd could have contained as many as 20,000 people, if only the men were counted, and each man had a wife and two children. Even by today's standards, this represents a huge throng.

While a lot of questions could have been asked about such a swarm of humanity, Jesus' question of Philip revealed the Savior's concern for their well-being. Jesus asked him, "Where shall we buy bread for these people to eat?" Notice that Jesus asked, "Where can we buy the food?" not, "How can we buy the food?" The Bible says, "He asked this only to test him, for He already had in mind what He was going to do" (John 6:6). As we grow closer to Jesus in following him, he sometimes tests us, and these tests develop our maturity and help us to align our life with his direction.

Philip's response revealed that he was more concerned about the "how" than the "where." Philip replied, "It would take a small fortune to feed them!" (John 6:7, NLT).

Seeing the hopeless impossibility of feeding the huge crowd, Philip answered the wrong question. Instead of trusting Jesus to provide the means to provide the food, he turned his attention to his own assumptions. His lack of faith prevented him from pursuing or proposing a solution. On his own, Philip must have felt intimidated and inadequate to help such a large group of people. He was about to see a different picture, however—and his own faith would grow in the process.

NUTRITION AND THE MISSION OF GOD

Admittedly, the task of reaching the world for Christ today seems overwhelming as well. At the time of Christ, there were less than 250 million people in the world. By 1650, there were 500 million. By 1850, there were 1 billion. By 1930, there were two billion. By 1975, there were 4 billion. Today, there are 6.8 billion people in the world. Those 6.8 billion people live in nearly 200 different countries. Half have never heard the Gospel of Jesus. Although figures vary, most estimate the world Christian population at around two billion, approximately one out of three persons globally. A recent Pew Research Center study of world religions showed that one out of every four citizens of planet earth is a Muslim. The statistics show 1.57 billion Muslims, nearly three quarters of a billion Hindus, 613 million Buddhists, and more than 150 million followers of other religions.[3]

As Andrew took an inventory of the hungry crowd, I am not sure he had a lot more faith than Philip, but when he heard Jesus asking about where to buy food, he started looking to see what was available. What he found was a good indication of the impoverished condition of this particular group of people. In a crowd of more than 20,000, Andrew only found one who had food. A young boy had brought his lunch—just a few pieces of bread and a couple of small fish. Can you imagine such a huge crowd with nothing but one sardine sandwich to feed them! No wonder Andrew remarked, "... but what good is that with this huge crowd?" (John 6:9, NLT)

Perhaps that is how we feel when we compare our resources with the needy billions in this world. We can look at the multitudes today and think the same things Andrew thought. What impact can we make with so little, in the face of such a great need for so many? In spite of the magnitude of the project, don't you think Jesus has a plan for reaching the lost people on planet earth? Will we engage in the mission of God? Will we start looking for organic and viral solutions that are within our reach? Followers of Jesus are called to be peacemakers, oppose injustice, feed the hungry, and heal the hurting. Such practical exercises of our faith cause it to grow organically even as we help Jesus to expand his kingdom.

The poverty of the people Jesus ministered to 2000 years ago is mirrored in multitudes of people in today's world. The majority segment of the world's population is children, and three out of four go to bed hungry every night. According to UNICEF, 25,000 children die every day because of poverty. Lack of clean water kills hundreds every day. Eighty percent of the world's population earns less than ten dollars per day.[4]

While these statistics about today's crises are difficult to fathom, journey back with me 2000 years. Can you imagine how the young boy in the story must have felt? I can see his mother packing his lunch for him with a stern warning not to misplace it or he would go hungry. When asked to share it with 20,000 people, he surely could have reasoned that it would be a waste among so many. But he was willing to share. Even though it wasn't much, he gave what he had. And compared with what others had to offer, his gift was both generous and sacrificial. Such acts of faith—living out our faith in community to serve others—causes our own faith to grow exponentially.

Though this story appears to be about the gifts of a young boy, it is really about the mission of God in this world. Jesus' compassion upon the multitudes of people and willingness to feed them was a physical analogy of what he came to do spiritually for lost human beings. His mission was to seek and save the lost (see Luke 19:10). "For God so loved the world that He gave His only begotten Son, that whoever believes in Him should not perish but have everlasting life" (John 3:16, NKJV).

Because one young boy was willing to give all, a miracle took place and a multitude was fed. Not only that, but enough leftovers remained for everyone to take some home. God can do way beyond our expectations when we sacrificially give to Him.

What if I gave all? What if everybody did? If every one of God's children was willing to give all, the multitudes of this world would be feasting on the bread of life. This world would be a different place, wouldn't it?

We often see the multitudes, but Jesus saw not only a multitude, but also individuals like Philip and Andrew and the boy with the lunch in the multitude. The job may seem impossible, but God can use just one person devoted to Him who will answer His call. Will that person be you? Jesus never would have told us to do something He wouldn't equip us to do. If you provide the availability, God will provide the ability and in the process, you will mature and grow. Many years ago, Edward Everett Hale (1822–1909) wrote: "I am only one, but I am one. I can't do everything, but I can do something. And what I can do, I ought to do. And what I ought to do, by the Grace of God, I shall do."

FOR FURTHER PERSONAL OR GROUP STUDY

1. Do you think most followers of Jesus today are under-nourished or over-nourished? Why?

2. Jesus said, "Man shall not live by bread alone." What do you think he meant by that? What is the correlation between our spiritual life and our physical life?

3. What do you think a diet balanced in spiritual nutrition might look like?

4. Read Hebrews 12:1–2. In a spiritual sense, do you need to lose any weight?

5. What areas of your life indicate a need for growth? How could you nurture that growth? Who could help you with that? What is stopping you from asking or moving forward?

6. Jesus' mission is to "seek and save the lost" (Luke 19:10). What do you think that means for you? Is the mission of God the most important thing in your life and/or church? How might a priority on God's mission help you grow personally, and your church grow corporately?

CHAPTER EIGHT

Struggles Grow Courage and Character

Since the late 1970s, I have enjoyed the hobby of raising bonsai, the Japanese art of growing miniature trees and shrubs. My collection of trees includes some that I started training back in those days. I learned the basic concepts of bonsai (pronounced "bone-sigh," which means *plant in a tray* as opposed to "bawn-zie" which means *may you live for a thousand years*) from a Japanese master in Portland, Oregon named Masahiro Furukawa. Masa didn't speak much English, but that did not stop him from showing me the various tools and techniques, and it did not stop me from observing his work or purchasing his supplies. Although you can learn about bonsai from a book, to become proficient you must see and do—someone has to both show and tell. That is exactly the way Jesus taught his disciples.

One of the lessons learned from bonsai is the truth that growth often comes following a time of severe pruning. To maintain the small dimensions of a tree that might be thirty, fifty or one hundred years old requires constant trimming of both what is above and below the ground. Contrary to what most gardeners would suggest, bonsai enthusiasts actually periodically prune the roots of their specimens.

Root pruning absolutely goes against the conventional wisdom of the most basic principle of horticulture. "Protect the rootball at all costs" is the mantra of gardeners and landscapers alike—and for good reason. When transplanting from one location to another, survival essentially depends upon keeping as much of the plant root intact as possible. Most people are incredulous when I tell them I regularly remove bonsai from the pot and prune the roots. "How do they survive?" is the common question.

They survive because trees organically grow by the constant growth of root systems to discover new sources of water and nutrients for the plant. Old roots become tough and less resilient, and the new roots have the tiny root hairs and fibers the tree uses to absorb the nutrients from the soil. A tree in a pot is not a naturally occurring phenomenon, and in time the roots will break out of the pot in search of nutrients, and without action, disaster occurs. Unless the roots are pruned periodically (sometimes annually, more typically every couple of years), the tree will eventually die because there is no room in the pot for further growth of new roots.

Root pruning involves amputation of about a third or more of the root system, removal of most of the old soil, and replacing the old with new. This is a dramatic action, as most gardeners could not imagine an established plant intentionally taken to the bare root stage, pruning those bare roots, and then replacing it in the same size or even smaller pot. Yet it is this extreme action on the part of the bonsai master that ensures the health and survival of the plant. Contrary to popular opinion, bonsai are not starved and stunted freaks of the natural world. They are intentionally grown to show the detail and image of great age and maturity, only in a miniature form.

Not only does the bonsai master prune the roots, but he prunes everything above the ground that does not fit his vision of how the tree should look. Branches that cross other branches, or grow in a direction contrary to his design must be pruned or trained to grow in the direction of his choosing. He does this by carefully wiring the branches and bending them gently, gradually, incrementally into the shape he has in mind. At other times, he applies weights to bend branches or in really tough cases, he will use a special clamp to create a bend or growth in the direction he envisions. Eventually, all of the pruning, bending, and shaping combine to create a bonsai masterpiece. And this process often takes a lifetime to achieve.

The spiritual applications are many. Certainly God does not want us to be a small imitation of the real thing. But he is the master, and he patiently works—bending, shaping, pruning, and tending us to create his masterpiece, a human being in the image of Jesus Christ. Notice the words of Jesus:

> I am the true vine, and my Father is the gardener. He cuts off every branch in me that bears no fruit, while every branch that does bear fruit he prunes so that it will be even more fruitful. You are already clean because of the word I have spoken to you. Remain in me, and I will remain in you. No branch can bear fruit by itself; it must remain in the vine. Neither can you bear fruit unless you remain in me. I am the vine; you are the branches. If a man remains in me and I in him, he will bear much fruit; apart from me you can do nothing. (John 15:1–5)

It is during this pruning process that I have learned a powerful lesson for life: sometimes the best growth comes during the winter, to heal the scars from pruning. Every Northern hemisphere gardener knows that the best time to transplant trees and shrubs is during the fall. That is because the roots will grow during the winter, giving the transplant a head start on growth for the coming spring. I know from observation of my bonsai that although there may be no evident signs of life in a deciduous tree during the winter months, a look beneath the surface shows that the roots have grown following a fall pruning. Not only that, but a closer examination reveals that many of the scars from pruning the branches have actually healed over or begun to heal over during the harsh winter months.

Even though we don't enjoy the process, we grow through suffering. God works to bring healing to our souls during the harsh months of winter suffering. Our struggles make us strong. This concept is revealed over and over again in the Bible. It provides one of the most basic organic principles: that our struggles make us stronger. Jesus fasted and endured temptation in the wilderness, but received the Spirit's power to overcome and became stronger through those things he endured.

A follower of Jesus struggles against his or her own sinful impulses, the temptations of the devil, and the challenges of living in a fallen world.

Virtually every type of struggle is illustrated in the life of Christ and in his interactions with his disciples and followers. Hunger, injustice, disease, poverty—every category of human misery can be seen in the Gospels. But along with the suffering comes the hope of redemption and the belief that we can become better and our faith can grow stronger during challenging times.

WEATHER

A farmer has many tools at his disposal and can control many things to create the perfect environment for growth. But he cannot control the weather. Freezing temperatures, scorching sun, drought, floods, tornadoes, hurricanes, rain, hail, and snow can all contribute to devastation of the crop. And the extent of the damage all depends upon the time of the year or stage of growth. Of course, tornadoes, droughts, floods, hurricanes, or other extreme forms of weather are unwelcome at any time. At other times, the particular weather needed depends upon what you are trying to raise or accomplish. When seeking conditions for making hay, a farmer will pray for nice warm, dry weather. His neighbor, wanting moisture for his corn or other crops, might pray for rain. I have always wondered how God responds to those prayers. I am sure he is not caught on the horns of a dilemma.

In his Sermon on the Mount, Jesus said, "You have heard that it was said, 'Love your neighbor and hate your enemy.' But I tell you: Love your enemies and pray for those who persecute you, that you may be sons of your Father in heaven. He causes his sun to rise on the evil and the good, and sends rain on the righteous and the unrighteous" (Matthew 5:43–45).

Jesus was not just giving a weather report, but rather sharing an important principle about relationships. We are to disregard the conventional wisdom of retribution when we are hurt; instead we are to "love our enemies." This was a revolutionary concept to Jesus' listeners, and practicing it requires a revolution in our thinking.

In his providence and grace, God provides weather for the benefit of all. The sun shines and the rain falls on both good and evil people. This concept strikes at the very heart of our human questions about suffering:

"Why do good people suffer bad things?" Books and sermons have been preached on the subject. The question is more universal than the answers, which are many. From the time of Job to the present, people are more concerned about the "why?" of suffering than any other question.

Perhaps Jesus wants us to understand that there is more to the picture than the frame we are watching at the present moment. Only God knows how our story will interact with other stories and how he can work to accomplish his purposes through both good and bad events and circumstances in our lives. Romans 8:28 should be more than a pat response thrown out as a religious platitude to people caught in the storms of life. "And we know that God causes everything to work together for the good of those who love God and are called according to his purpose for them" (Romans 8:28, NLT). This should be considered an essential principle of spiritual formation, a bedrock anchor of faith when the winds of adversity prevail.

Followers of Jesus grow organically as they struggle through life's unpredictable weather. Do you ever think of how often various types of weather enter our conversation as metaphors for our description of life's circumstances? "It struck me like a bolt of lightning!" we might say when a sudden solution to a pressing problem appears. Or we might ask, "Who rained on your parade?" when a friend looks seriously discouraged. Back in the 1970s, John Denver crooned about *Sunshine on My Shoulders*, and Karen Carpenter sang, *Rainy Days and Mondays Always Get Me Down*. Their reference to the weather immediately resonated within people's spirits, because they automatically knew what they were talking about. The language of weather is a universal language.

WEEDS

In the thirteenth chapter of Matthew, following the parable of the sower and seed, Jesus told another story—this one about weeds:

> Jesus told them another parable: "The kingdom of heaven is like a man who sowed good seed in his field. But while everyone was sleeping, his enemy came and sowed weeds among

the wheat, and went away. When the wheat sprouted and formed heads, then the weeds also appeared.

The owner's servants came to him and said, 'Sir, didn't you sow good seed in your field? Where then did the weeds come from?' 'An enemy did this,' he replied. The servants asked him, 'Do you want us to go and pull them up?' 'No,' he answered, 'because while you are pulling the weeds, you may root up the wheat with them. Let both grow together until the harvest. At that time I will tell the harvesters: First collect the weeds and tie them in bundles to be burned; then gather the wheat and bring it into my barn.'" (Matthew 13:24–30)

In both this story and the Parable of the Sower, Jesus mentions how weeds compete with the intentionally sown crops, often choking them out in a struggle for available moisture and nutrients. The book of Genesis tells us that weeds are a result of the fall of man (see Genesis 3:17–19). As any gardener will tell you, the battle for survival against the weeds is a never-ending struggle despite the most valiant efforts to keep them out. Constant vigilance is the price of a weed-free garden.

In the story above, commonly known as the "Parable of the Wheat and the Tares" (tares are weeds), Jesus advocates the strategy of just letting the weeds grow until harvest. That certainly goes against the conventional wisdom. Several years ago my wife's grandfather stopped by for a visit and took a look at my garden. "Son, don't you own a hoe?" was his wry observation. My pitiful excuse that I had been busy the past week did not do much to stand up to the evidence that the weeds were overtaking my garden.

The tares or weeds mentioned in this story closely resembled the wheat plant, and because the wheat was already sown thickly, to try and pull out the weeds would almost certainly be an exercise in futility. Only by waiting until the time of harvest could you easily distinguish between the wheat and the weeds. Then, it would mean extra work, but they could be separated.

Remember this parable is about God's kingdom, not about weeds growing in an individual life. Perhaps Jesus was helping us to recognize the importance of not judging people by their appearance, but by their fruit. This may have been a reflection back on something he mentioned in the Sermon on the Mount, "Watch out for false prophets. They come to you in sheep's clothing, but inwardly they are ferocious wolves. By their fruit you will recognize them" (Matthew 5:15–16)

Weeds growing in your own personal life are another matter. They can rob you of nutrients, and if you are not careful, they can take over your life. Farmers practice a variety of methods for weed eradication, some more environmentally friendly than others. While a hoe works, it is labor intensive and often impractical for large fields. So more extreme measures are taken, such as fire, biological controls (bugs that attack the weeds), herbicides (chemicals), or planting weed-resistant crops. Something must be done because weeds and thistles, like bad habits, multiply rapidly, and they can destroy your crop and profits.

They can also be toxic. On the farm, we were vigilant in removing weeds, especially weeds like tansy ragwort, commonly known as tansy or ragweed. Tansy looks deceptively like a wildflower with its pleasing yellow daisy-like flowers. Yet the flowers are the most toxic part of the plant. It is deadly to cows and horses, and to a lesser extent goats and sheep. Its toxic properties remain if baled with hay or included in silage, so it poses a real threat to livestock as well as humans unless it is eradicated from the field. Following Christ means controlling the weeds in your life as they can be both destructive and deadly.

PESTS AND DISEASES

A variety of pests and diseases threaten crops and livestock on a farm. The Bible promises this reward for those who tithe, "'I will prevent pests from devouring your crops, and the vines in your fields will not cast their fruit,' says the Lord Almighty" (Malachi 3:11). Since biblical times, pests and diseases have been a problem and continue to threaten the farmer's livelihood.

We have grown accustomed to hearing about epidemics of swine flu or avian flu, so it should come as no surprise to us that farmers guard against outbreaks of disease in their livestock or crops. Good nutrition and a healthy environment are the first lines of defense against any disease, whether on a farm or in a home. At times, extreme measures such as medication or isolation are necessary. At the very least, precautionary measures should be carried out to include sanitation procedures and regular handwashing.

God cares about not only our physical, but our spiritual health as well. So we must guard against the diseases that can destroy our souls. Human tendencies toward selfishness, lust, greed, envy, or revenge are among the reasons for the Ten Commandments. Before actions like adultery or murder take place, they are generally plotted in the heart. The Bible is full of precautionary advice in the form of life principles, which a follower of Christ disregards at his or her own peril. Verses such as this one encourage us to practice preventive care from the diseases of the soul: "Above all else, guard your heart, for it affects everything you do" (Proverbs 4:23, NLT).

Rats, mice, or other vermin may not be very big, but can multiply rapidly and create a great deal of damage. On our farm, rats were a particular problem, because of the ready availability of feed and habitat in our chicken houses. Rats reach reproductive maturity in three months, and have litters of six to twelve young, born about three weeks after mating. A female rat can have four to six litters per year. They are omnivores and will eat virtually anything, dead or alive. Eradication requires extreme measures utilizing traps, poison and, on our farm, dogs trained to dig and destroy.

Even furry critters that look cute can be very destructive. I have long battled with deer that love to eat my flowers and roses. Bunny rabbits left nothing but stems on my neighbor's garden this year. And I heard from a friend about a flock of wild turkeys that demolished more than an acre of ripe grapes overnight.

I once watched from a distance as a coyote killed one of our neighbor's sheep, ignoring my yells and threats because he knew I was too far away to do him any harm at the moment. Jesus told many stories about shepherds and sheep such as this one:

> Therefore Jesus said again, "I tell you the truth, I am the gate
> for the sheep. All who ever came before me were thieves and

robbers, but the sheep did not listen to them. I am the gate; whoever enters through me will be saved. He will come in and go
out, and find pasture. The thief comes only to steal and kill and
destroy; I have come that they may have life, and have it to the
full. I am the good shepherd. The good shepherd lays down his
life for the sheep. The hired hand is not the shepherd who owns
the sheep. So when he sees the wolf coming, he abandons the
sheep and runs away. Then the wolf attacks the flock and scatters it. The man runs away because he is a hired hand and cares
nothing for the sheep. I am the good shepherd; I know my sheep
and my sheep know me." (John 10:7–14)

In Scripture, human beings are frequently compared with sheep, and
it's not a particularly flattering comparison. Isaiah said, "All of us have
strayed away like sheep. We have left God's paths to follow our own"
(Isaiah 53:6, NLT) Sheep are not known for their intelligence. Left to their
own devices, they get into trouble. They require the constant care and
keeping of a shepherd.

One of our neighbors raised sheep, but did not really exercise much
care of them, leaving them to fend for themselves in the abundant pastures in the Willamette Valley. Because they were typically left to fend
for themselves, they were subject to danger, like the coyote attack I witnessed. One spring I noticed that some of his sheep had a distinctively
green tint to their wool. I did not think it was a St. Patrick's Day decora-
tion, and upon closer examination noticed that there was actually grass
growing on their backs. I knew full well that sheep are not smart enough
to figure out a plan for self-grazing, hence I determined that they must
have rolled around in the grass in the fall, and grass seeds had become
embedded in their wool. Because of the abundant spring rains in the
Willamette Valley, the seed had sprouted and started to grow right on
their backs. Had their owner had them sheared as would normally be
done to care for them in the spring, this would not have occurred. (This
was a case where the shepherd of the sheep did not exhibit much more
intelligence than the sheep themselves.)

In contrast, Jesus called himself, "the good shepherd." He protects his sheep from the wolf, and cares for them in a safe environment. Like David's description of the Lord in Psalm 23, he leads us, feeds us, protects us, and generally cares for us. Peter spent a lot of time with Jesus. Therefore, the fisherman learned a lot about sheep. He wrote, "For you were like sheep going astray, but now you have returned to the Shepherd and Overseer of your souls" (1 Peter 2:25). In 1 Peter 5:4 he describes Jesus as, "the Chief Shepherd." Peter also encouraged believers to: "Be self-controlled and alert. Your enemy the devil prowls around like a roaring lion looking for someone to devour. Resist him, standing firm in the faith, because you know that your brothers throughout the world are undergoing the same kind of sufferings" (1 Peter 5:8–9).

GROWING THROUGH SUFFERING

Charles H. Spurgeon, born in 1834 and one of the most influential ministers in the nineteenth century, began his pastoral ministry while in his early twenties. His rise to fame as a speaker who appealed to the masses was phenomenal. Overall, he was one of the most famous preachers that ever lived, leading thousands of people to faith in Jesus Christ. During his lifetime he was one of the most recognized men in London.

Charles Spurgeon's career as a pastor could have ended on a disastrous night in October of 1856 and we would never have heard from the 22-year-old minister again. On that night he was preaching in the famed Royal Surrey Music Hall in London to a crowd of thousands when someone shouted "Fire," and started a stampede for the doors. There was no fire, but seven people died in the chaos and nearly thirty were seriously injured.

Spurgeon was greatly distressed and despondent over those circumstances, because he was already going against conventional wisdom by holding religious services in a public building. But because his friends stayed by him and prayed for him, he returned to preach again in the Royal Surrey Music Hall with great success. Spurgeon served for thirty-eight years as pastor of the Metropolitan Tabernacle in London. During that time he saw the church grow to over 20,000 members, the very first true "megachurch." His sermons filled forty-nine volumes that are still studied and used by ministers today. He once said:

> Stars may be seen from the bottom of a deep well that cannot be discerned from the top of a mountain: so are many things learned in adversity which the prosperous man dreams not of. We need affliction as the trees need winter, that we may collect sap and nourishment for future blossoms and fruit. Sorrow is as necessary for the soul as medicine is to the body. The path of sorrow, and that path alone, leads to the land where sorrow is unknown.[1]

As we stay close to Jesus, we learn to grow through times of struggle or suffering, and are protected from the many pests that seek to destroy our souls.

FOR FURTHER PERSONAL OR GROUP STUDY

1. How important are courage and character in your life? How would you rate yourself in these areas?

2. Have you ever had a chance to look at a bonsai tree up close? If not, find a picture of one on the internet. Is there anything about the tree or process of shaping it that seems applicable to your life, particularly your spiritual growth?

3. "Along with suffering comes the hope of redemption and the belief that we can become better and our faith can grow stronger during challenging times." Explain why you agree or disagree with that statement.

4. How important is it to have friends or a faith community to support you during the storms and challenges of life? How would you describe the strength of your support system? What might you do to strengthen it, or support others who are struggling?

5. In our natural lives, how do things like weather, weeds, pests, and diseases remind us of the need for faith in God's goodness?

6. "As we stay close to Jesus, we learn to grow through times of struggle or suffering, and are protected from the many pests that seek to destroy our souls." What are some ways that you stay close to Jesus?

CHAPTER NINE

Seasons Provide the Rhythm of Life

L ooking at old sepia-toned or black and white family photos one gets the impression that everyone was older back then. The lack of color makes every scene take on a monotonous ambiance reminiscent of damp, shadowy, cold winter days. No matter that the people portrayed may have been younger and more vibrant than we are. Nor does it matter that the photos may have been taken during spring or summer. The people from the past seem as distant and stoic as the expressions seen on many of their faces. Seasons come and go; someday our present reality will be another person's ancient history, too.

The concepts of time and seasons are ingrained in farm life. On a daily basis, schedules are determined by chores that need to be accomplished in order of importance. From milking cows to hoeing the garden, there is a time in the daily schedule for everything and those tasks vary, depending upon the season of the year. In fact, farm tasks are more defined by season than any other category. For Jesus and his disciples, their activities seemed to be scheduled more by the season than on a daily or weekly schedule. Reading their activities on the pages of the Gospels, one does not get the sense that they had a daily schedule at all. The Jewish concept of time was far more seasonal, linked to festivals and harvests, and less confined to a clock. Although the New Testament mentions specific hours of the day in a few places, people did not watch the clock as we do—in fact they had no clocks to watch!

As a boy, we always planted a garden in spring. I can remember several times going out to the garden and looking for signs of germination after planting the seeds. I am sure I uprooted and killed many beans and kernels of corn in my quest to see if the seeds were really going to grow or not. Patience has never been one of my virtues!

Henri Nouwen may have been thinking of people like me when he wrote:

> A seed only flourishes by staying in the ground in which it is sown. When you keep digging the seed up to check whether it is growing, it will never grow fruit. Think about yourself as a little seed planted in rich soil. All you have to do is stay there and trust that the soil contains everything you need to grow. This growth takes place even when you do not feel it. Be quiet, acknowledge your powerlessness, and have faith that one day you will know how much you have received.[1]

When it comes to spiritual formation, time is our ally and friend. It takes time to form into the image of Christ—that is one of the components that cannot be altered. There is great wisdom from learning to wait and read the signs of the seasons—to cooperate with them for optimum growth. The writer of Ecclesiastes wisely wrote, "There is a time for everything, a season for every activity under heaven. A time to be born and a time to die. A time to plant and a time to harvest" (Ecclesiastes 3:1–2, NLT).

Farmers also realize the perennial nature of certain crops. In the dead of winter, you might never know that an apple tree will be laden with apples in September, unless you understood the seasonal nature of fruit. It would be a grave mistake to assume the tree was dead or worthless just because it was in a season of dormancy. Spiritually, we may go through dormant seasons as well; that does not indicate death, but more likely a season of rest in preparation for a season of harvest.

God has placed rhythm in nature. You can hear it in the croaking of frogs in the spring, the clap of thunder and splattering raindrops during a summer shower, the rustle of leaves in autumn's wind and the chattering of our teeth from winter's icy chill. The seasons provide a rhythm to life, cycles by which we are prompted to do more than merely survive or exist, but to grow.

The seasons of life do more than just help us mark the time. It's true; some people seem never to accomplish more than listening to the ticking of the clock or marking the hours until quitting time. For others, though, the hours and minutes mark a schedule for accomplishing meaningful goals. The seasons of life are indicators of time, helping us chart the course of our God-given destiny. They keep us from getting bogged down for long in any one site; they spur us with the necessity of movement and change, whether we like it or not.

Farmers understand the importance of meaningful work, and the necessity of seasons, cycles, and patterns that establish important boundaries and order:

> Industriousness, independence, fair play, and honesty, traits that gain meaning and substance through hard work, comprise the central features of the traditional farmer's work ethic. Hard work for the farmer is more than keeping occupied. It is the basis for his or her respect and self-esteem. A farmer's esteem attaches both to work itself and the goals that work fulfills. These goals, short and long term, are pursued with great personal sacrifice to comfort and leisure. Farmers and their families endure working in the heat of summer, the bitter frost of winter, laboring during harvest from five in the morning till after dark, loading hay by searchlight, milking at midnight and dawn, driving long miles to market, and caring for family, farm, and animals in every kind of adverse weather. Farm work is physically exhausting. Yet, farm families have the satisfaction of calling the land their own and of watching nature procreate under their loving care. If not all farmers achieve this ideal level of respectability through dedicated work, it is the standard by which their peers judge them.[2]

CHRONOLOGY OF SPIRITUAL DEVELOPMENT

The Apostle John was known as the "beloved disciple" because of his closeness to Jesus. For three years, John was part of the inner circle of Jesus' most trusted disciples. Years later, he wrote specifically about spiritual formation. No doubt having been both personally discipled by Jesus and having ministered to others as a church leader during the ensuing years helped form his perspective on spiritual growth. He lists three categories of maturity as follows:

> I write to you, dear children, because your sins have been forgiven on account of his name. I write to you, fathers, because you have known him who is from the beginning. I write to you, young men, because you have overcome the evil one. I write to you, dear children, because you have known the Father. I write to you, fathers, because you have known him who is from the beginning. I write to you, young men, because you are strong, and the word of God lives in you, and you have overcome the evil one. (1 John 2:12–14)

First, he speaks to children. The original Greek word in the text is, *teknion*, meaning "an infant, children, or darlings." According to the *Strong's Bible Dictionary*, the implication of the word is "new or young Christian converts."

John provides two identifying characteristics of "children." Most importantly, they have had "their sins forgiven." Next, they "have known the Father." This makes clear the implication that he is speaking to new believers, or people who have recently come to know the Lord Jesus Christ as their personal Savior.

A person who crosses the line of faith and trusts in Jesus Christ will become literally "born again," regardless of chronological age (see John 3:3). Born-again people receive forgiveness of sins and a new start. New believers in Christ need the same care, attention, and proper nourishment as a newborn baby. Abandonment at birth can have disastrous consequences, because their primary need is to be nourished by prayer and Scripture as they learn to follow Jesus, coached or mentored by fellow believers.

The second category John addresses (although not in order) is "young men." This comes from the Greek word *neaniskos* which literally means, "a youth or anyone under the age of 40." This group is identified by the following characteristics:

- They have overcome the evil one (vs. 13).

- They are strong (vs. 14).

- They are knowledgeable in, and living by, Scripture (vs. 14).

- They have overcome the evil one (vs. 14) – repeated perhaps from verse 13 to emphasize their victory in spiritual conflict.

"Fathers" are identified as the final category of maturity. This comes from the Greek word, *pater* which literally means "father or parent." John identifies this person as one who "has known Him who is from the beginning." A father then, is any person who has grown to an age of spiritual maturity and is able to parent or disciple others.

John was in a unique position among the apostles to discuss cross-generational discipleship. Tradition tells us that he was the only one of the original twelve disciples to die a natural death, and do so at an old age, following his exile to the Isle of Patmos. No doubt the isolation of that exile made him keenly aware of the importance of a community of faith. During his lifetime he experienced and noted the value of spiritual growth over time. Older believers need younger believers in a community of faith. The elderly need the youth just as much as the youth need their elders in a healthy family or church.

As a person matures in spiritual formation, what are some signs of Christian maturity? Although not intended as a conclusive list, here are a few benchmarks:

- A love for God and love for God's people (passion for God, compassion for people).

- An attitude of service above self, portrayed through action.

- Regular habits of spiritual discipline: prayer, meditation, Bible study, fasting, silence, etc.

- Active involvement with a community of believers.

- Evidence of the fruit of the Spirit in daily living.

- A willingness to share your faith in Jesus Christ with others.

- Humility balanced with leadership; evidenced by a willingness to teach others along with a willingness to learn.

Chronological age does not determine spiritual development or maturity. As Richard Foster noted, intentionality is a key component leading to growth. If one desires to grow, maturity is possible while following Jesus. All it takes is time.

TIME

The Bible tells the stories of numerous young people shining for God in the spring of life. Mary, David, Samuel, Joseph, Daniel and Timothy are a few examples. However, the opportunity to serve is not limited to the young. Moses was eighty when God called him, but he never used his age as an excuse. Michelangelo, known for spending four years painting the ceiling masterpiece in the Sistine Chapel while lying on a scaffold during his thirties, was still composing poetry and designing structures in his eighties. For sixty years, John Wesley rose at 4:00 A.M. and for fifty years, he preached at 5:00 A.M. He traveled more than 250,000 miles by horseback, preached more than 40,000 sermons and wrote 400 books. He learned ten languages. At the age of eighty-three he was annoyed that he could not write more than fifteen hours a day without hurting his eyes, and at eighty-six he was ashamed that he could not preach more than twice a day. He complained in his diary that there was an increasing tendency to lie in bed until 5:30 in the morning! These men all made good use of the time afforded them.

In the Old Testament, all units of time were based on observation and experience. By far the most important and basic unit of time for the Jews was the day. Days were easy to count. Days made up weeks, weeks made up months, and months made up years. We find more than seven hundred uses of the word "time" in the Bible.

In the New Testament, the Greek words for time are *chronos* and *kairos*. *Chronos* has the meaning of "a measure of time" or chronological time. *Kairos* means "a moment in time," or what we might call a window of opportunity.

Time is a wonderful gift from God. (Maybe that's why now is called "the present.") Time is our greatest, our most abundant resource because we all have the same amount of it, twenty-four hours every day. No amount of worrying or wishing will change that fact. Time is available to all. And it is valuable. That's why most people get paid in proportion to the amount of time spent on the job. Whether by the hour, day, week, month, or year, our time is valuable.

In our present dimension of living, time is a certainty. Einstein factored it into equations. We expect that just as yesterday was, today is, and that there will be a tomorrow. But because of our mortality, we cannot be certain that tomorrow will come for us, or of what it might bring.

I don't know a thing about quilting, yet it doesn't take a lot of creativity or sewing skill to appreciate the beauty of a patchwork quilt. An intriguing thing about most old quilts is that they were made using small blocks of leftover fabric. In the same way, even small blocks of time, if spent on worthwhile projects, can help form us into beautiful works of art, disciples who are moving closer to Jesus.

Organic spiritual formation occurs when we make the best use of the time we have. Ephesians 5:16 says, "Making the most of every opportunity" (NIV). Other translations say, "redeeming the time." In a few minutes a day you could learn a foreign language, read a book, hone your musical skills, explore a new job skill or hobby, or become physically or spiritually fit. Most people who do these things don't have the luxury of large blocks of time in which to accomplish their goals. Francis Bacon said, "Begin doing what you want to do now. We are not living in eternity. We have only this moment, sparkling like a star in our hand—and melting like a snowflake."

Daily determination to walk with Jesus, to pray and study your Bible, will reward you with spiritual growth and bring you to new levels of faith. In about fifteen minutes a day you can read through the Bible in a year. An octogenarian recently told me, "I've been a Christian for years and never thought I could read through the whole Bible; it seemed so big.

I'm glad I started a regular Bible reading schedule this year and now I'm nearly through. If I could do it, anyone can."

You can change the future by praying today. Prayer can accomplish what worry cannot do. Corrie ten Boom said, "Worry does not empty tomorrow of its sorrow; it empties today of its strength." Pray not only for your own needs, but also for the needs of others. In so doing, you develop compassion and gifts of mercy and can change yourself in the process.

The psalmist prayed this prayer, and we would do well to follow his example: "So teach us to number our days, that we may gain a heart of wisdom" (Psalm 90:12, NKJV). The New Living Translation renders this verse: "Teach us to make the most of our time, so that we may grow in wisdom."

For a moment think of time as a seed. Today we are sowing what we will reap in some future tomorrow. This is biblical, for Paul wrote, "A man reaps what he sows" (Galatians 6:7). In context, this verse warns against sowing bad seed through dishonorable or sinful actions. Many people sow wild oats and then pray for God to send a crop failure. However, it also applies to sowing good seed. The challenge lies in patiently awaiting growth and maturation of the good seed. Shakespeare expressed what we all desire in Macbeth:

> If you can look into the seeds of time,
>   and say which grain will grow, and which will not, speak then to me[3]

Once used, our allotted time can never be replaced. To one and all, rich or poor, big or small, the account of time is eventually exhausted. To some, it happens swiftly and unexpectedly. Like the twin towers of the World Trade Center, you may have every reason to believe that you will last for many, many more years. Then the unexpected happens, and in one tragic moment your account is empty. Your friends and family mourn your loss. But nothing they do will be able to bring you back or change those final seconds.

To most, though, the account is gradually depleted, as a healthy bank account that provides a comfortable living for years, but whose withdrawals eventually exceed the deposits. Like a bucket of water with a small leak, the full account slowly erodes, in an almost unnoticeable fashion. Eventually it is completely empty. And an empty bucket is still an empty bucket, whether its contents were suddenly lost by a swift kick, or gradually leaked out over a long period of time.

When you are sixteen, you think you will live forever. A thirty-year-old seems ancient. After all, your sixteen-year-old brain reasons: "They have already lived almost twice as long as I have." But before you have a chance to blink twice, your teenage years are gone, and half a decade goes by.

You are now twenty-five, and beginning a career and family. You barely have time to cut the birthday cake when you hit the big three-oh. After all, time flies when you're having kids! And wasn't it just a few days ago you were saying something about thirty-year-olds and ancient history?

You hit the forty-year mark and realize it hits back with the shocking realization that half of your life has been spent. But you can easily rationalize, "I still have another half to go." And so, like a compulsive shopper with an extended line of credit, you go on, not thinking much about the coming day of reckoning—when you'll eventually reach your credit limit and the bills must be paid.

At half a century you wonder why young people think you are "old." Why, only yesterday you graduated from high school and got married and started a family. But reminiscing about the past does not change the present. Every look in the mirror is a reality check. The application for AARP membership sits on your desk. As hard as it is to accept, you know you are not a kid any more, and your body tells you so every day.

Then come the sixties. At retirement most people wish for health and strength to enjoy life, and thankfully many people do. But some folks discover those two items were lost in the pursuit of something else along the way. You could spend the next several years wishing you had made better use of your time and taken better care of yourself when you were young.

At seventy-five, eighty, or even eighty-five you look back and simply cannot explain where all the time has gone. It seems like only yesterday your children were young, you were busily involved in your career, and thinking life, as you then knew it, would last forever. Today, a few faded photographs and scrapbooks in the attic are all that remain of that era. While you may be surrounded by loving family members and friends, it just doesn't seem possible that those days will never be again.

At ninety or ninety-five you are painfully aware of your mortality. Your aches and pains are like the ticking of a clock, a steady reminder that the minutes are passing by, just as life seems to be passing you by. Many at this stage of life do not understand the younger generation. Perhaps they long since gave up trying. Direct marketers and advertisers target you with mailings and phone calls about Medicare supplements or extended care facilities. You hesitate to buy green bananas, thinking, "Why take the chance?"

Your account is nearly empty and you know it. So you measure the future in days, not decades. Over the past several years, you've attended far more funerals than weddings. So many of the faces from your past are now only memories. Like the last grains of sand trickling from the top half of an hourglass, you can see the remnant of your friends and peers disappearing from sight. And like those grains of sand, your generation will soon be gone. You are constantly aware that at any moment the next grain of sand might be you.

I do not mean to try and scare with dramatics, because whether we are nine or ninety, none of us have a guarantee of more time. The Bible says "Why, you do not even know what will happen tomorrow. What is your life? You are a mist that appears for a little while and then vanishes" (James 4:14). The truth is, every one of us is never more than a heartbeat or a breath away from eternity.

On his deathbed, the wealthiest person in the world might be willing to exchange his billions of dollars for something you probably take for granted, more time. Suppose he offered you $100 for another minute—or $1,000 for another hour—or how about a million dollars for a month—or even a billion dollars for a year? If you were able to exchange a part of your lifetime for his money, would you do it? No matter how serious his offer, the fact is he cannot buy another moment in time at any price. And his future is not yours to change.

Seeing our dilemma, at the right moment in history, Jesus Christ left eternity and entered into our dimension of time. Galatians 4:4 says,

"But when the time had fully come, God sent his Son, born of a woman, born under law, to redeem those under law, that we might receive the full rights of sons" (NIV).

Jesus came to provide something for us that we could not provide for ourselves. Regardless of our wealth or social status, He came to provide something which money cannot buy. He came into time, from eternity, in order to bring eternity unto us. Although it seems complicated, it is as simple as John 3:16–17, "For God so loved the world that He gave His only begotten Son, that whoever believes in Him should not perish but have everlasting life. For God did not send His Son into the world to condemn the world, but that the world through Him might be saved."

The old motto I've read on the walls of countless homes is true, "Only one life, will soon be past. Only what's done for Christ will last." Jesus asked, "For what will it profit a man if he gains the whole world, and loses his own soul?" (Mark 8:36, NKJV). At the end of the day, and at the end of the journey, everything invested in our spiritual formation through all the seasons of life will be worth it.

FOR FURTHER PERSONAL OR GROUP STUDY

1. Would you describe yourself as a patient or impatient person? How does your answer make you feel, and how does it affect others?

2. What does the New Testament writer James (James 1:1–4) say about patience and spiritual growth?

3. What does Hebrews 10:35–36 say about patience and God's promises?

4. How would you describe the season of life you are in right now? What is God doing in your life to help you grow during this season?

5. How would you describe your spiritual maturity? Where would you like to be spiritually, and what will it take for you to get there?

6. "Organic spiritual formation occurs when we make the best use of the time we have." What could you do to become a better manager of the time you have? How might that help you or others grow spiritually? Why not find a friend to pray with you about this and help you be accountable in this area?

PART FOUR

COMMUNITY

CHAPTER TEN

Spiritual Formation Requires a Journey

Life is a journey. I don't know about you, but the best travel experiences of my life have not been solo trips. A journey is best experienced with others. A community of friends can help smooth out the rough places in the road, provide lively conversation, and keep you on track toward the destination.

Jesus began a three-year journey with his disciples with the simple words, "Follow me." He did not begin by telling them where he was going, and at times they must have wondered about the destination. Of course, the final destination is important, yet the real growth takes place while on the journey. That is the way it was for Jesus and his disciples, and so it will be for us. They journeyed without a roadmap, schedule, or compass—they simply followed. At the core, this defines an organic process, one that is held together with the fabric of relationships.

Jesus did tell his disciples what they would become. "Come, follow me," Jesus said, "and I will make you fishers of men" (Matthew 4:19). This had to do with their identity, their character, and ultimately, their occupation. These guys were fishermen. Jesus got their attention by appealing to where they were in the journey of life, and giving them a vision for a higher purpose. He was saying, "Listen, you've been fishing for fish, a humble but honorable occupation. If you come along with me, I will teach you how to become fishers of men." He changed their perspective from a very parochial one—providing a service within their own neighborhood—to a context where they would make a difference for God that could change the world, one person at a time.

JOURNEY AND FAITH

Every human being is a traveler on the journey of life. Everyone can relate to this metaphor. My early life on the farm did not involve much travel beyond the boundaries of our own state. Yet I understood the concept of a journey, and often dreamed of traveling beyond the farm fences that defined my boundaries for the first eighteen years of my life.

The human story is a story of migration—people on the move. Church life and history is rich with language about the journey of faith. The route is filled with mountains and valleys, settings that provide rich metaphors for the joys and challenges of life. Who hasn't experienced a high mountaintop experience of victory on one day and the next day been plunged deep in the valley of despair? People are often referred to as pilgrims or even strangers in Scripture, prose, song, and verse. The writer of Hebrews describes the heroes of faith with these words, "These all died in faith, not having received the promises, but having seen them afar off were assured of them, embraced them and confessed that they were strangers and pilgrims on the earth" (Hebrews 11:13, NKJV).

On the journey of faith, there are no first or second class travelers, but Jesus guides each person on a unique path with and toward himself. No one is said to have "arrived" in this life—the arrival is yet to come. And there are challenges and trials along the way. At times we feel lost and alone. At other times we lose patience because we are frustrated by the amount of traffic on the journey of life. Growth occurs along the journey as we experience the tensions, dilemmas, and choices between the here and now and the yet to be in God's kingdom.

TRAVEL ARRANGEMENTS

An observant reader of the Gospels will notice that Jesus and his disciples were seldom stationary. They were continually on the move. Although their journeys never took them beyond the borders of first century Palestine, the geography of the area is diverse, from the snow of Mount Hermon to the desert oasis of Jericho, near the lowest place on planet earth, the Dead Sea. The people they met along the way were as diverse as the climate zones and geography they encountered.

Not only were Jesus and his disciples on the move, there was a certain randomness in their travels. They didn't always take the shortest route to get to their destination, and they sometimes seemed to backtrack or go in circles. At other times they seemed uncertain of their destination altogether. Not that there wasn't intentionality in the direction Jesus took. He was led by the Spirit and went exactly where they were destined to go. But to the casual observer, their travel itinerary might have seemed somewhat haphazard, not what one would expect a travel agent or event planner to assemble.

Likewise, the process of spiritual formation may not follow a specific itinerary or step-by-step process. I appreciate having a GPS in my car that gives me turn by turn navigational instructions. It generally gets me to my destination on time, and even provides the estimated time of arrival. Prior to the days of GPS, Google Maps, or Mapquest, I relied on low-tech devices that have proven themselves over the centuries—a roadmap, and sometimes a compass. I also relied upon directions from people who had taken the journey before me. Often their input made the difference and helped me avoid missing a landmark or taking a wrong turn. Their experience and testimony gave me more confidence that I was on the right path.

DON'T FORGET TO PACK ...

For the Christ follower, the essentials for the journey of spiritual formation are definitely low-tech—really more suited to an organic approach than a modern mindset. Since we don't have Jesus in the flesh to lead us or give us verbal commands, we need to use a few basic tools to stay on course. Our roadmap is the Bible. It is not exactly a step-by-step manual leading to spiritual formation, but when followed and applied, the Word of God certainly makes a difference in your life. Likewise, the Holy Spirit provides a sort of inward compass, steering us away from the pitfalls in the journey and intentionally guiding us in making our next steps. Also, we can be encouraged by fellow travelers who have journeyed ahead of us. Their testimonies, mentoring, or coaching encourage us and help us stay on the right path.

If the process of spiritual formation is low-tech and multifaceted, it is also possible that Christians go back and forth between stages of growth as part of their journey. At times we make forward momentum, at other times we return to re-visit basic landmarks, lessons, and matters of faith that we may have forgotten or lost familiarity with. Organic spiritual formation could often be described as a journey of two steps forward followed by one or two steps back, in a somewhat random sequence.

DISCIPLES ON THE JOURNEY

It is interesting to note how many times Jesus actually mentioned the concept of a journey or trip in his teaching and preaching. In Matthew chapter ten, Jesus sent his disciples out on a journey—their first mission to spread the Gospel. Rather than offering them a long list of suggested supplies for the trip, somewhat surprisingly Jesus said:

> Do not take along any gold or silver or copper in your belts; take no bag for the journey, or extra tunic, or sandals or a staff; for the worker is worth his keep. Whatever town or village you enter, search for some worthy person there and stay at his house until you leave. As you enter the home, give it your greeting. If the home is deserving, let your peace rest on it; if it is not, let your peace return to you. If anyone will not welcome you or listen to your words, shake the dust off your feet when you leave that home or town. (Matthew 10:9–14)

How would you like your boss to send you on a business trip with those instructions? "...What? no luggage, no credit card, no money, no hotel reservations, no meal stipend, no per diem? How will this work? I'm supposed to just depend upon the kindness of strangers? You've got to be kidding!" Jesus' instructions sound more like the ethos of the "Jesus People" of the 1960s and 70s than the corporate structure of today's Christian church. What Jesus proposed, indeed *ordered*, seemed illogical. What about planning, organization, and preparation? Aren't those valid concerns?

From reading the context of these verses, we see how Jesus painted his disciples a picture of the future. He showed them what he wanted in the previous verses, and then he sent them on the mission. The mission was the important thing:

These twelve Jesus sent out with the following instructions: "Do not go among the Gentiles or enter any town of the Samaritans. Go rather to the lost sheep of Israel. As you go, preach this message: 'The kingdom of heaven is near.' Heal the sick, raise the dead, cleanse those who have leprosy, drive out demons. Freely you have received, freely give." (Matthew 10:5–8)

Though the vision and mission were clear, the procedures for carrying out the mission were sketchy. True, Jesus did give some specifics. But weren't those specifics just a few abstract thoughts? After all, how long would it take them to preach the message, "The kingdom of heaven is near"? Was that just the title; wasn't there something more to say?

Jesus made his instructions purposely abstract, instead of giving concrete, step-by-step directives. He wanted his disciples to emulate what they had already seen him do. Now it was their turn and he was empowering them to do it their own way—with some guidelines and boundaries. Leaders grow organically when they are empowered to actually lead and use their own gifts in ministry.

A CHANGE IN TRAVEL PLANS

Too often, we do the opposite. We set up rules, guidelines, policies, and procedures, but often provide little in the way of vision or helping disciples focus on the mission of God or empowerment for service. Almost anyone can work on an assembly line, doing the same thing they are told to do over and over again. This may have worked well in the twentieth-century corporate structures, but it is not working well today to engage younger generations of leaders.

Recently, J.R. Kerr recently made this observation:

My generation is hungry for something more than the 15 principles for building a better team or the 21 reasons why you should be a servant leader. They are not content filling a role on a task force for church growth. They are hungry for more. They want a voice. They want influence. They are a generation that isn't content receiving a vision; they want to be part of shaping and creating the vision. My generation believes in open source influence.[1]

Open source collaboration has changed the way we process technology and information. Wikipedia is a prime example of the power of allowing ordinary users to make a contribution, not only a select few in the hierarchies of academia or business. In a word, leadership is influence, and in God's kingdom open source influence or leadership describes an organic process for allowing disciples to collaboratively work together to fulfill the mission of God. In the process, those leaders mature and develop their own leadership skills. That seems to be what was happening as Jesus sent off his disciples on ministry assignments with such unusual marching orders. He empowered ordinary people to do extraordinary things. As they went and learned by experience, their own leadership skills were forming and they were developing spiritual maturity along the way. Shouldn't we embrace that strategy in making disciples and doing ministry? After all, we're living in a world where thousands of user-developed iPhone apps exist because of the same strategy that Jesus employed.

By sending forth the disciples with sketchy details, Jesus was teaching them another, more subtle, lesson as well. By extension, he was teaching the same lesson to us in the twenty-first century church. If nothing else, he was teaching them to live by faith. He wanted them to experience the journey of faith mentioned in Hebrews chapter eleven. This faith journey is an organic process, based upon networking and following the leading of the Holy Spirit. It can be criticized, scrutinized, and analyzed but at the end of the day it cannot be categorized or strategized or synthesized into a program that we can authorize and sanitize into a specific method of ministry or spiritual growth.

Though we long for a certain way of doing things, a clearly right way and a clearly wrong way, such black and white decisions rarely exist in ministry. That is why it is dangerous to equate methods or styles of ministry with a particular style or organizational structure. God is immutable, and unchanging, but our methods and often language must change to engage the current population.

Even Jesus used different strategies for ministry under different circumstances and with different people. Look at the variety of ways Jesus healed people. To some he asked for a sign of faith. For others, he provided healing without any confession of faith. A healed leper was given instructions to go show himself to a priest. Others were sent on their way without any reference to a priest. One woman was healed by touching the hem of his garment. To the blind man in John chapter nine, he made mud out of dirt and spit, and then applied it to his eyes. He then instructed him to go wash his eyes in the Pool of Siloam where he was healed. Those looking for a pattern or method are hard pressed to find one besides the obvious mission that Jesus is a healer of broken people and souls.

We are accustomed to working with a specific plan or procedure that starts with listing the tools and resources necessary for the job. In the business of spiritual formation, human beings provide the raw materials and each one requires a unique plan to become all that God intended. This plan involves living according to God's purposes, and in so doing, accomplishing his will. We learn the details of the plan along the way, as we walk with Jesus on a daily basis through the journey of life.

In 1916, Robert Frost published a poem titled, *The Road Not Taken*. It helps to illustrate the fact that life really is a journey and that we have a variety of options. "Two roads diverged in a wood, and I— / I took the one less traveled by. / And that has made all the difference."

Sometimes the little choices we make in life that really do make all the difference. Had it not been for a mutual friend, or the fact that I chose to attend a particular church youth event as a teenager, I might never have met my wife. Naturally, we seldom realize the importance of those little choices and decisions at the time. Because we never see more than a small snapshot of the entire roadmap at any one time, we are prone to be shortsighted. That makes it even more important to stay close to Jesus and walk with him so he can show us the way. It can be a tall order.

The Apostle Paul reflected on this challenge in 1 Corinthians 13:12. He wrote, "Now we see things imperfectly as in a poor mirror, but then we will see everything with perfect clarity. All that I know now is partial and incomplete, but then I will know everything completely, just as God knows me now" (NLT). Here he contrasts our present blurred vision with the future clear revelation in heaven. When we see Jesus Christ face-to-face, we will see everything else with clarity. Even in this life, the more clearly we see Jesus, the more clearly we will understand the meaning of the here and now.

The Easter story provides the foundation for our faith in Jesus as the resurrected Son of God. Before the resurrection came death and despair. Jesus' followers were scattered and shocked. You can read Luke's version of the story beginning in Luke 24:13. All of Jerusalem was in an uproar. The disciples of Jesus were in hiding. There was serious talk of disbanding their group. They were about ready to close the door on the New Testament church for the last time. Little did they know that they were really only forty days away from the grand opening of the church doors on the Day of Pentecost!

Without Jesus, they couldn't go on. Their hopes were crushed, their dreams shattered. As far as they could see, their leader was gone. But was he? Strange reports from some of the women and a firsthand account by Peter told of an empty tomb, grave clothes lying wrapped as though the body had just evaporated from them, and an appearance by angels announcing a resurrection.

As two friends walked on the road to Emmaus (a distance of about seven miles from Jerusalem) they discussed the situation. We know the name of one, Cleopas (possibly a male form of Cleopatra). His name meant "the glory of being called a father." A name like that would identify him as a leader. Obviously both Cleopas and his companion had been closely associated with Jesus and the twelve disciples. Perhaps they were part of the larger group of seventy that Jesus had sent out.

We don't know why they were walking to Emmaus. Maybe they lived there. Maybe they were escaping Jerusalem for fear of losing their own lives. Maybe they just wanted to walk and talk and try to sort things out in their minds. Whenever we have problems, it helps to talk things over with a friend. The resurrection of Jesus Christ is the greatest miracle and the greatest event in history. Yet, from day one it has generated a lot of questions—for many people more questions than answers. That's the way it is with miracles. Reason asks questions. Faith simply believes the impossible is possible.

Cleopas and his buddy were walking along and asking questions— probably rhetorical questions. They may or may not have expected answers, but they needed to ask the questions. Their questions represent the dilemmas many of us face in the journey of life:

- "What are we going to do now? What is going to happen to us?"

- "If He did rise from the dead, how did he do it?"

- "Why did this happen to a good guy like Jesus? He didn't deserve what he got."

The Bible says "they communed together and reasoned..." (Luke 24:15, KJV). The Greek word for "reasoned" is *suzeteo* and means "make a thorough investigation." These guys wanted to know what was going on. They were posing the questions of suffering that everybody asks at one time or another. First, we want to know "What happened?" or "How did this happen?" This is the quest for details. We want to understand fully the whole story. Like hearing the news of a friend's sudden death, we want to understand how it happened. Was it an accident or a sudden illness? We want to know who, what, when, and where. Details of information will be passed back and forth to satisfy our need to know.

Second, "Why did this happen?" This is a more profound question, and one that consistently persists. Once we know how, we want to know why. The "why" questions are always the most difficult. They often defy solution. We search for reasons. Like Cleopas and his buddy, we look for answers, even though they often can't be found in the here and now.

- "Why did Jesus return to Jerusalem if He knew people wanted to kill him?"

- "Why did Peter deny Jesus?"

- "Why did Judas betray Jesus and then kill himself?"

- "Why didn't Jesus stop the people who were killing him?"

- "Why didn't we all stick together?"

When we are troubled, it is helpful to remember that Jesus walks with us on our journey of life. He is never distant or far away. While these disciples were walking along and trying to figure things out, Jesus drew near to them. During troubled times we may think God is a million miles away. Panic sets in when we feel abandoned. We don't usually make good decisions when we are in a state of panic or fear. And fear makes a poor lens for viewing life. It distorts reality and magnifies problems. It makes God appear to be far away while trouble appears to be next door.

Jesus is as close as the mention of his name. The Bible is full of promises about God's nearness and comfort during our times of sorrow and grief. The journey may get rough at times, but Jesus will strengthen our faith as we recognize his presence and trust the promises of Scripture:

- God is our refuge and strength, an ever-present help in trouble. (Psalm 46:1)

- God did this so that men would seek him and perhaps reach out for him and find him, though he is not far from each one of us. (Acts 17:27)

- For He Himself has said, "I will never leave you nor forsake you." (Hebrews 13:5, NKJV)

- ... surely I am with you always, to the very end of the age. (Matthew 28:20)

- Be strong and of good courage; do not be afraid, nor be dismayed, for the Lord your God is with you wherever you go. (Joshua 1:9, NKJV)

If you focus on problems, you'll miss seeing the solution, even if it is right beside you. Jesus Himself walked right up to those travelers on the Emmaus road and they didn't recognize Him. Even though the object of their despair and the solution to their trouble had just appeared miraculously out of nowhere, they viewed him as a stranger. We generally look for answers in the familiar, in the things we know and recognize, the things that fit in our pre-determined box, not in the strange or unfamiliar. We sometimes overlook great treasures because they seem plain, simple, or familiar to us. You never know when you will run across something valuable in your journey through life. Sometimes solutions come to us cleverly disguised as problems. What we perceive as hard work is often really the opportunity to succeed and see God's faithfulness and provision for us.

Jesus always cares and his presence changes everything. Not only did Jesus come near to them and walk with them, He listened to them, and we can overhear their conversation:

> "You seem to be in a deep discussion about something," he said. "What are you so concerned about?" They stopped short, sadness written across their faces.
>
> Then one of them, Cleopas, replied, "You must be the only person in Jerusalem who hasn't heard about all the things that have happened there the last few days." "What things?" Jesus asked. "The things that happened to Jesus, the man from Nazareth," they said. "He was a prophet who did wonderful miracles. He was a mighty teacher, highly regarded by both God and all the people. But our leading priests and other religious leaders arrested him and handed him over to be condemned to death, and they crucified him. We had thought he was the Messiah who had come to rescue Israel. That all happened three days ago. Then some women from our group of his followers were at his tomb early this morning, and they came back with an amazing report. They said his body was missing, and they had seen angels who told them Jesus is alive! Some of our men ran out to see, and sure enough, Jesus' body was gone, just as the women had said." (Luke 24:17–24, NLT)

A caring friend will always take the time to listen. Jesus had all the time in the world. Can you imagine how silly it must have seemed to Jesus as they described a situation he understood a lot better than they? He had perfect understanding, yet he was willing to listen to their dilemma. He will listen to each one of us as well. Once again we can integrate Scripture into our journey of faith:

- Call unto me, and I will answer thee, and show thee great and mighty things, which thou knowest not. (Jeremiah 33:3, KJV)

- "Now glory be to God, who by his mighty power at work within us is able to do far more than we would ever dare to ask or even dream of—infinitely beyond our highest prayers, desires, thoughts, or hopes" (Ephesians 3:20, TLB)

- Cast all your anxiety on him because he cares for you. (1 Peter 5:7)

On the road to Emmaus, Jesus took the time to offer an explanation to these friends. "Jesus quoted passages from the writings of Moses and all the prophets, explaining what all the Scriptures said about himself" (Luke 24:27, NLT). Jesus is a gentleman. He listened and he explained. They had an engaging conversation. As they walked, they approached their destination. He did not invite himself in for dinner. He will not force himself on anyone. He will respond to an invitation, though. He waits patiently for each of us to invite him into our heart. He says, "Behold, I stand at the door and knock," (Revelation 3:20, NKJV).

Cleopas and his friend invited Jesus in and he joined them for a meal. Jesus wants fellowship with us. He wasn't angry with them. He loved them and was concerned for them. As Jesus blessed the dinner bread, they suddenly understood. Their eyes were opened and they immediately knew who he was. Along with that revelation came something unexpected. God is always doing things we don't expect. He vanished out of their sight. But even though they couldn't see him with their physical sight, their spiritual eyes were opened. That is what happens when we journey with Jesus; we walk by faith, not by sight.

An encounter with Jesus changes everything. They had seen the Lord and their emotions went from confused sadness to elation. Excitedly, they told each other how their hearts had felt strangely warm as he explained the Scriptures to them as they walked down the road.

When we can't clearly see the road ahead because our vision is blocked by tears or a tangled web of weeds, we must focus on Jesus. Once we see him, he gives us vision for the road ahead and shows us the way. When Jesus accompanies us on the road less traveled, it makes all the difference.

FOR FURTHER PERSONAL OR GROUP STUDY

1. "A journey is best experienced with others." What do you think about that statement? Would the answer be different for a person who is introverted, as compared to an extrovert?

2. Can you think of the three most influential people in your life's journey of faith? What did they do to help you grow in your faith? How could you pay it forward by helping others in the journey?

3. In terms of geography, what do you know about your family's history of migration? How has that history had an impact the person you are today?

4. Do you feel confident in the direction your life is heading? If you keep going in the same direction, where will it lead? Where would you like to be?

5. Why do you think it was difficult for the two disciples on the Emmaus road to recognize Jesus? What are the things that prevent us from recognizing God's face and work in our lives?

6. "When we can't clearly see the road ahead because our vision is blocked by tears or a tangled web of weeds, we must focus on Jesus." Read John 20:20. What needs to change in order for you to focus on Jesus more clearly on a regular and consistent basis? How will doing so enhance your life and nurture your own spiritual growth?

CHAPTER ELEVEN

Growing Through Community

*I*t *Takes a Village* was a best seller during the 1990s, and for a variety of reasons the book was not too popular in evangelical Christian circles. Be that as it may, the title reflects a truth about spiritual formation. An orphan left alone to fend for himself cannot become a fully formed follower of Jesus Christ. It takes a village—a family and community engaged in helping that individual develop to his or her fullest potential.

Growing up on a farm, I lived in a village, a small rural community where we knew our neighbors. The local church I attended during all of my growing up years never had a regular attendance of more than 250 people, and often hovered around the 100 mark. Although I sometimes longed for anonymity as a child (because the mothers around town acted as field agents who were always ready to report my mischievous behaviors to headquarters), there was something comforting and reassuring about knowing that I was cared for by a large extended family and could seek refuge among friends and neighbors under any circumstances.

Jesus Christ was born in a small village. Bethlehem seemed an unlikely spot for a King to be born. The prophet Micah foretold the birth of Christ approximately 700 years before it took place, "But you, Bethlehem Ephrathah, though you are little among the thousands of Judah, yet out of you shall come forth to Me the One to be Ruler in Israel, whose goings forth are from of old, from everlasting" (Micah 5:2, NKJV).

Compared with Rome, the center of the civilized world at the time, or even Jerusalem, the city of Zion, Bethlehem must have seemed insignificant, a true "hick town" known primarily for its sheep and bread. Perhaps you have felt like Bethlehem, "little among thousands." We all struggle with feelings of inferiority as we wrestle with life's complex challenges. That is precisely why we need to be close to others; to encourage us and serve as a catalyst for us to move forward, to help us understand that together is to be better than we could ever be alone, and to work together to accomplish more than we could while working solo. The preacher of Ecclesiastes wrote, "Two people are better off than one, for they can help each other succeed" (Ecclesiastes 4:9, NLT).

There is something about the community context in which we live that can evoke strong emotions ranging from pride to embarrassment. As a child, I was often ashamed of living on the farm, particularly when we were spreading manure on the fields and the foul essence was blowing in the wind toward the neighbors and everyone who happened to be driving by at the time. At times I longed for cement, loathing the muddy roads and fields around the farm that made riding a skateboard or bike, or playing basketball, impossible. A city with concrete sidewalks and blacktopped basketball courts seemed like paradise to me. And I often wished for anonymity, thinking how marvelous it would be to live in a big city, where a boy could just blend into the crowd and do what he wanted, without the fear of being observed and recognized around every corner.

With the wisdom of years come different emotions than those experienced in youth. Today I am grateful for my childhood home and community—mud, manure, and all. Because it was there I learned the great lessons of life: how to work, collaborate, see a job through to completion, use innovative techniques to make repairs, and make do with what I have. I learned how God works through a community of people, in seasons, storms, and soil to develop roots of faith that serve as a firm foundation for building a life. My embarrassment has melted into civic pride—a good kind of pride that is tempered with humility and keeps life in perspective by valuing things truly important. In essence, this describes character, and it is a byproduct of spiritual formation, developed within a context of community.

Sadly, for several generations the evangelical church viewed their unchurched neighbors as the "enemy," and fearing the spread of worldliness into the church, erected barricades on many levels. This often resulted in a gatekeeper mentality, scrutinizing those who might wish to visit or come in, and carefully training insiders to avoid contact with outsiders to avoid contamination which they feared could ultimately lead to the insiders backsliding or losing their faith by joining in sinful activities with their "heathen" neighbors.

Not long ago I visited with a pastor in Southern California who had recently come to lead a church situated in a changing community context. Neighbors from a variety of ethnic groups now resided in the area and far outnumbered the Anglo population who originally built the church and made up most of the congregation. When the new pastor arrived, he was met by a group of members who advocated building a high iron fence all around the church property and stationing a security guard at the parking lot. These church members seemed particularly concerned about the influx of students from the high school next door who liked to relax or smoke on the church lawn. He also was warned about a nearby neighbor who had been so troublesome that the church had actually obtained a restraining order to prevent him from trespassing on the church property.

Taking his cues from Jesus, instead of the fearful congregants, the pastor was able to talk them out of the fence, and instead encouraged the members and youth pastor to work with the students and the administration at the high school. They now have an open door of ministry at that school. He reached out to two pastors of ethnic congregations that needed a place to meet, and now three thriving congregations share the ample facilities. The pastor took the initiative to build bridges of friendship to the neighbor who had been served a restraining order, and eventually invited him to church. He is now following Jesus and on Easter Sunday he brought more visitors to the church than any other single person.

Through Jesus, a church or individual can make a difference in a community. This only happens, though, when that church or individual actually engages in the life of the community. Not only does isolation in a holy huddle stifle spiritual formation because of stagnation, it blocks the work of the Holy Spirit in drawing people to Jesus who need him the most. Most people in twenty-first century western society are not going to come to church because we have great worship, music, or preaching. They are not exactly looking for those things. They do value authentic relationships and community, however. So every church and pastor should be asking the question: "If our church were removed from this community today, would anybody in the community notice or care?" If the answer is "no," then something should be done to change that reality.

Jesus was not only born in a small village, he was raised in another small village. Nazareth provided the cultural and social soil in which Jesus grew. And it was not the ideal place. When Jesus began his public ministry, one of his potential disciples asked, "Can there any good thing come out of Nazareth?" (John 1:46, KJV). Apparently Nazareth did not have a reputation for producing outstanding civic leaders, and was not making much of a difference either. Jesus changed all that.

It was in Nazareth that Jesus spent his formative years. One of the key verses of the New Testament describes Jesus as a youth of twelve or so, "And Jesus grew in wisdom and stature, and in favor with God and men" (Luke 2:52). Notice the four components of growth in Jesus' life. These components are the basis for building a healthy life. Jesus grew intellectually, physically, spiritually, and socially. They correlate with the verbs applied to every human: being, thinking, feeling, and doing. Let's take a closer look at these components and see how the community context affected them.

WISDOM: INTELLECTUAL GROWTH

It is unlikely that Jesus had any formal education beyond that offered by his local Nazareth synagogue. After beginning his ministry at the age of thirty, Jesus returned to his home synagogue one Sabbath day and publicly read from the book of Isaiah. Luke records the response of the people, "The eyes of everyone in the synagogue were fastened on him, and he began by saying to them, 'Today this scripture is fulfilled in your hearing.' All spoke well of him and were amazed at the gracious words that came from his lips. 'Isn't this Joseph's son?' they asked" (Luke 4:20b–22, NIV).

Later in his ministry, Jesus was in Jerusalem preaching and teaching in the temple. John records this response from the leaders, "The Jews were amazed and asked, 'How did this man get such learning without having studied?' (John 7:15) It was generally assumed that Jesus, an itin-erant preacher from Nazareth of Galilee, was a man without formal edu-cation in the accredited schools of Jerusalem.

The word Luke used (Luke 2:52) for wisdom is the Greek word, *sophia*. This word conveys the concept of wisdom, or the application of knowledge, either in a worldly sense or a spiritual sense. The truth is, Jesus was taught not only by the local rabbis to read and write, but by the Holy Spirit and through communion with his Heavenly Father. As the incar-nate Word of God, spoken of in John chapter one, Jesus embodied the Scriptures. Yet as a human being, he studied them and interpreted them flawlessly. His preaching left his listeners amazed because he preached with the passion and certainty of the author.

The point for us to remember is this: if Jesus studied the Scriptures and lived them out in a practical way, so should we. If Jesus grew in *sophia*, so should we. A lack of formal or higher education should not be a hindrance to organic spiritual growth. The key to growing is to have a desire or passion for faith and growing closer to God, resulting in deeper roots of faith. Nor should an abundance of education hinder our spiri-tual progress. All who come to the Lord must do so in a spirit of humility, willing to learn. In the words of a psalm, "Reverence for the Lord is the foundation of true wisdom. The rewards of wisdom come to all who obey him" (Psalm 111:10, NLT).

Writing on this subject, James encourages, "If any of you lacks wisdom (*sophia*), he should ask God, who gives generously to all without finding fault, and it will be given to him" (James 1:5). James wrote from firsthand experience, because he was a half-brother of Jesus. Having grown up in the same home and community as Jesus, James was in a unique position to encourage us to seek after the Lord, the true source of wisdom.

MATURITY: NATURAL GROWTH

According to Luke's (2:52) description of Jesus, he also grew in "stature." The Greek word Luke used here is *helikia*, meaning maturity in age or size. Because Jesus was not only fully God but also fully man, he was subject to the normal growth patterns of human beings. He was born as a baby, not as a fully grown adult. The infant Jesus was wrapped in diapers or swaddling cloths, not adorned in the robes of a king. He had to learn to crawl, walk, speak, be potty-trained, and do all the other things a child does during the growing-up years. Jesus lost his baby teeth, went through puberty, and experienced everything a normal human male experiences in the physical and emotional sense.

Consider the overwhelming confidence and risk of Jesus' Heavenly Father in allowing his only begotten Son to be born under the primitive conditions present in the first-century Middle East. Mary and Joseph were given a sacred trust; they had no professional or practical preparation for raising the Son of God. Jesus was born in a culture where there would be no vitamins, virtually no awareness of the causes of disease, no antibiotics, and little available in the way of formal education. People regularly died of causes that can easily be treated today. Most common people were never more than a meal or two away from starvation. There were no insurance policies, no supermarkets, no democratic political processes for the Jews in first-century Palestine. Yet within the parameters of a small community like Nazareth, without the trappings of modern society, the Son of God grew and matured.

SPIRITUAL MATURITY: THE GROWTH OF THE SOUL

Organic spiritual formation integrates the spirit, soul, and body toward the process of maturity. The Apostle Paul prayed, "Now may the God of peace make you holy in every way, and may your whole spirit and soul and body be kept blameless until that day when our Lord Jesus Christ comes again" (1 Thessalonians 5:23, NLT). Generally speaking, the "soul" refers to that part of us that goes beyond the physical realm. The soul encompasses the mind (our intellect or cognitive function), the will (our free moral agency), and our emotions.

Spiritual formation occurs only when all three parts are addressed; it is biblically holistic.

Paul uses the Greek word *pneuma* for spirit, a word typically meaning wind. Our human spirits are eternal, and they distinguish us from the rest of God's creation. Genesis 2:7 states, "The Lord God formed the man from the dust of the ground and breathed into his nostrils the breath of life, and the man became a living being." Man is not just an animal. Human beings are different because God has breathed the breath of life into us. We are spiritual beings.

The human spirit is difficult to define and impossible to identify or prove scientifically. Yet we know it exists—it's like the wind that we feel but cannot see. And like the air we breathe, the Spirit brings life to our weary souls. Just as we cannot exist without air to breathe, when the spirit departs from the body, we die (see James 2:26).

We can see the holistic alignment of all of this as we explore the subject a little further. Modern medicine has provided us with information that helps us understand the important relationship of systems within the human body. We now understand things that the ancients were not aware of. We know that there is a direct correlation between the flow of oxygen into our lungs and the passage of that oxygen into our blood that in turn circulates throughout the body and provides sustenance to every organ, including our brains.

The heart is often associated with the soul in Scripture. In 1 Thessalonians 5:23 Paul uses the Greek word *psuche* which is translated "soul" in English. Like the word for spirit, this word also conveys something to do with the respiratory system or breath. We typically think of the soul in terms of cognition, or the mind, as *psuche* forms the root of our English word psychology. Just as the heart circulates life-giving blood throughout the body, so our character is sustained by our soul. Our mind, will, and emotions can either be under God's reign, or our own. We have the capacity for good or evil, and our actions are formed by the intents of the heart.

Luke (2:52) explains that Jesus grew in "favor with God." The Greek word used for favor is *charis*, a term that encompasses the idea of a gift, grace, or graciousness. In his humanity, as Jesus matured, he became ever more gracious. To do this, he had to empty himself of his sovereign right as God, with all the attributes of God, and humble himself as a human being. He did this to show us that it is possible to develop spiritually, to grow in grace, in spite of and in the midst of our humanity.

Paul wrote, "Your attitude should be the same that Christ Jesus had. Though he was God, he did not demand and cling to his rights as God. He made himself nothing; he took the humble position of a slave and appeared in human form. And in human form he obediently humbled himself even further by dying a criminal's death on a cross" (Philippians 2:5–8, NLT).

Our thoughts are mere speculation, but do you think Jesus as a child, adolescent, or teenager was always kind, loving, and understanding of his siblings? Do you think he ever got impatient? Was he an emotionally mature adult inhabiting a thirteen-year old body? Luke seems to indicate that even for Jesus, specifically because of his human nature, spiritual and emotional development was a process that happened over time.

Even more remarkable is the fact that Jesus developed this graciousness without a human mentor, without formal instruction outside of the local synagogue, without books on leadership or spiritual growth, without Sunday school curriculum, and without a youth pastor or planned activities. Despite its lack of amenities, Jesus did find in Nazareth everything he needed to develop and grow spiritually.

RELATIONSHIPS AND SOCIAL DEVELOPMENT: GETTING ALONG WITH OTHERS

Finally, Luke (2:52) describes Jesus growing in "favor with men." The Greek word used for "men" is *anthropos*. Jesus was an anthropologist—a student of human nature. He was born into an ideal classroom for such research. Every aspect of the human condition—the good, the bad, and the ugly—could be found in the cast of characters that come to life in the Gospels.

God made us to be social creatures. At the very beginning of creation, God said, "It is not good that man should be alone" (Genesis 2:18). Organic spiritual formation takes place within the crucible of human relationships. While it may be a challenge to get along with yourself, the real test of your patience and character comes in your relationships with others. Living in isolation prevents us from developing the strength that only comes when our souls are exercised. In isolation, one's mind, will, and emotions might seem to be on an even keel. But put a person in a room full of opinionated and demanding people, and the balance is upset. Under those circumstances, people may resort to either silence or violence.

Community affords the opportunity for our greatest growth, or our greatest failure. That is why the New Testament makes such a point of spelling out principles about relationships. More than forty-one times in thirty-seven verses, New Testament writers use the term, "one another." Here is a well-known example from Jesus, "A new command I give you: Love one another. As I have loved you, so you must love one another. By this all men will know that you are my disciples, if you love one another" (John 13:34–35).

I believe the best context for obeying Jesus' command for community is within the local church, because Jesus is the hope of the world and the church, which he founded, best expresses that hope in the present world. The New Testament Greek term is *ecclesia,* from which we get words like ecclesiastical. Ecclesia or church in the New Testament sense of the word means literally, "a group of called-out ones." Jesus has called us and we have responded to his call.

If we only keep engaging in life, with all its complexities, struggles, and relationships, we too will grow. Jesus grew intellectually, physically, spiritually, and socially—and was in no hurry to do so. Jesus waited until he was thirty years old to begin his public ministry. The process of natural growth and maturity for a human being is a slow process and takes years to complete. The process of spiritual formation takes even longer. Becoming like Jesus requires a lifetime commitment to follow him. In that process, we must recognize and embrace our humanity, learning to bring our human-ness or "flesh" as Paul describes it (see Romans 7 or Galatians 5), into alignment with Jesus and his Word. Perhaps the best way to do so is in community, with a small group of fellow pilgrims.

THE HEART OF COMMUNITY: SMALL GROUPS

Jesus started with a small group of twelve. This was expanded to become a larger group of seventy, and eventually it grew exponentially.

There is a sense of intimacy within a small group of twelve that cannot be experienced in a group of seventy. And while it is possible to know everyone in a group of seventy, it becomes difficult to know everyone in a group of seven hundred, and virtually impossible to know everyone in a group of seven thousand. There is a reason the median church in America has an average attendance of about seventy.[1] That number is sustainable, and it is easy for people to know one another and feel comfortable. (It is also easy for them to become inwardly focused, and for guests to feel like outsiders—another reason why evangelism can become stifled in a smaller church setting and why the smaller church may remain small.) Even though most small congregations use the motto, "we are a friendly church," the truth is they are most friendly to each other, and often ignore guests or make them feel uncomfortable because those guests don't know the unwritten rules, dress code, language, or ethos of the group.

Larger congregations are learning that the key to sustained growth is in helping people assimilate through the use of small groups. This is where the real transformation and spiritual formation can take place, not in a megachurch service setting. In terms of sharing life and growing with a community of believers and seekers, there is no substitute for a small group. From a practical standpoint, it is much easier to stay in contact with a few people than a large number of people. Schedules being what they are, the larger the number of people in a group, the greater potential for not being able to connect at an agreed-upon time and place. Organic spiritual formation occurs best in small groups for a variety of reasons. Let me list a few:

1. First, it is the method Jesus used with his disciples. It is biblically based and sustainable. It can work virtually anywhere you can gather two or three or more in his name.

2. It does not require a large budget or building to host a small group on a regular basis. Most homes work fine, or space can be found in a local restaurant, coffee shop, community building, or church building.

3. Small groups most closely resemble a family, a context almost everyone is familiar with. The most basic lessons of life are learned within a family unit, and the same is true for the lessons of spiritual formation.

4. Change is most observable in a small group. Details of life and progress in faith—things like prayer needs and answers—are more readily shared in a small group.

5. Like the ever-present "mothers" acting as secret agents in the small community where I grew up, accountability works best within a small group context where people can ask if you followed through on your promises from a week before. Without accountability of some kind, spiritual formation cannot be measured or even defined.

6. Authenticity becomes the norm as people in a small group won't always accept the answer of "fine" when asked, "How are you doing, really?" Masquerades generally don't work in a small group of people who know you well. It is not easy to hide in a small group.

7. Finally, small groups meeting in a community context generally have shared values and experiences by living in the same local environment. They can work together and grow together by corporately and individually showing the character of Christ within the community. They can work on common goals of education, health, safety, peace, or justice and be a positive influence for Jesus Christ.

While we all need times of solitude, we were made for community. We all need friends, people to walk beside us in sunshine or shadows. And while you could play a game, eat dinner, take a vacation or even move furniture by yourself, together is always better.

When a group or team of people gets involved in a discussion or a project, they create a dynamic energy that is not present when a person is doing something alone. Synergy is the term used to describe the group dynamic where the sum of the parts working together is able to accomplish more than any of them could accomplish working separately. That's why there is such potential power when a family or church or community really starts working together, organically.

THE LEADING EDGE OF COMMUNITY: ONLINE SOCIAL NETWORKS

I have already written briefly about Facebook and Twitter. Technology is constantly changing the way we communicate and relate as human beings. I purchase and read books on my Kindle. In 2010, the iPad introduced a whole new generation of easily portable and user-friendly tablet computers, with unlimited applications and networking possibilities. Especially for younger generations, social engagement increasingly takes place online, not to mention smartphones.

Online churches, Bible study groups, and forums create opportunities for conversations about spirituality. Bloggers freely express their thoughts, allowing a window to the world for their opinions and beliefs. How this will impact the way churches engage people in becoming fully developed followers of Jesus Christ remains to be seen. What seems apparent is the fact that people are already accessing this as a way and means of spiritual formation, by becoming part of a larger community of believers online.

While writing this book I have been serving as an advisor for a doctoral student who is working on her dissertation for a major Christian university. She is researching the impact of online education on spiritual formation. For many Christian colleges and universities with online course offerings, this is question is of major importance for reasons of credibility and accreditation.

Is it possible to grow spiritually when you are not actually face-to-face with another human being? How effective is a virtual environment as a catalyst for spiritual growth? Once published, her research should provide us with some concrete data on these important questions, and the preliminary data suggests that it is possible to grow spiritually via an online community.

Just yesterday I received a call from a dear friend in another state. He asked for prayer for his infant grandson, facing major surgery. While assuring him of our prayers, with his permission I was able to multiply those prayers by posting the request online and leveraging my relationships with thousands of people on Facebook and Twitter. Multitudes of online friends took the time to notify me that they were praying for an infant child they have never met, illustrating how online communities of faith can provide more than just virtual participation in spiritual practices. I spoke later with my friend, and he expressed gratitude for the tangible comments and prayers by a vast body of believers, who may never meet face-to-face, but who have a spiritual connection through a felt need and mutual faith in the Lord Jesus Christ.

FOR FURTHER PERSONAL OR GROUP STUDY

1. How would you describe your community? How connected are you to it, or to your neighbors? What would you like to change about either of those things?

2. What type or size of community are you most comfortable in, and why? How do you think that affects your interactions with other people, or even your choice in a church or community of faith?

3. Which things in your community assist you in your spiritual growth, and which things are a hindrance to your spiritual growth?

4. How should churches make a difference in their broader communities? What is your church doing to make a difference?

5. Are you involved in a small group of some kind within your church or faith community? How would you describe your experience? What are the elements that help you and others to grow in their faith?

6. What do you think about the reasons listed in this chapter why organic spiritual formation occurs best in small groups?

7. What guidelines do you think a person should follow to avoid potential problems in social networking and make it a positive experience?

CHAPTER TWELVE

Polished Apples, or Unpolished?

Back on the farm, apples were a favorite crop. We never grew them for sale, but only for our own use. Our apples were grown organically, without any chemical sprays or commercial fertilizers. Early on, I learned when eating an apple to take a good look at every bite, and I was only alarmed when I found half a worm—because that meant I had probably consumed the other half!

When I started taking horticultural classes in high school, I learned all about chemical sprays and commercial fertilizers that would eliminate the worms and diseases that disfigured our apples. My dad was of the old school, however, and wouldn't budge on that point. I personally think he was more opposed to spending money on chemicals or fertilizer than he was in favor of organic farming methods. He was a practical man and after all, we had plenty of manure on the farm for fertilizer, and we could easily cut the wormy or bad parts out of the apples before we made applesauce, cider, or pies. Besides, I had to admit they generally tasted better than the store-bought varieties.

My ag teacher in high school taught us about chemical sprays for orchard use, and also about the importance of marketing to the consumer. I mentioned my dad's reluctance to spray our apple trees, and he said, "Your dad could never sell those apples in the store. Nobody wants to buy a wormy or diseased apple." He was right. All the apples in the store in those days were waxed, polished and red—fit for the teacher's desk. Still today, commercially grown apples for the consumer market (unless they are organically produced) are pampered, sprayed, washed, waxed, and polished before they make it to the grocery shelf. No wonder they cost $3 a pound or more these days! What consumers don't realize is that those are only the best, the primo apples from the tree. Their siblings ended up as apple juice, applesauce, apple pie, dried apples, or some type of apple filling for a donut or dessert.

In contrast, organic apples, even those sold in the grocery store, are generally a bit smaller, and they lack the eye-popping polish of the commercial variety. The typical organically grown apple would not win any prizes for appearance. It must be accepted as it is, worms, warts, blemishes, and all. That won't appeal to some people, but for me, an apple is not an object to be placed in a fruit bowl for observation; it is a fruit to be consumed—and I prefer the organically grown variety for both aroma and taste, hands down.

Imperfect apples grow in the real world. Jesus was the perfect Son of God, but he gathered some un-perfect apples around him, including at least one very bad one. After three years of training, they still were not very polished—not much of his perfection had rubbed off on them. What we learn from this is that the process of organic spiritual formation cannot be accomplished by a well-oiled institutional machine with its polished people and programs. Organic spiritual formation occurs in the real world, with worms, warts, diseases, and all. The transformation from a bad apple to a good one is what Jesus is all about. He works to polish out our imperfections, even though we don't always look too polished in the process.

The modern world is fascinated with polish. Slick magazines, glitzy advertising, neon lights, patent leather shoes, candy-apple-red trucks with chrome ornamentation, sparkling jewelry, and shiny cases for our gilded trophies reveal our enthrallment with glamor and glitter as indicators of success. We don't have to look very far to see that this same fascination has crept into the church.

With the advent of television ministries in the 1950s, many pastors and church leaders felt the need to improve every component of the worship service in order to compete with growing religious media voices.

For most small congregations, the competition was definitely an uphill battle. And it is a battle that existed mainly in the minds of leaders, as there really is no way of comparing the impact or effectiveness of a radio, television or media "pastor" in fostering spiritual formation with the impact or effectiveness of a local church and pastor.

During my growing-up years, I can remember mom and dad watching Oral Roberts, Rex Humbard, and Jerry Falwell on Sunday morning television before our own church services. Later, when I became a pastor back in 1977, I faced Sunday morning congregants who had already heard singing accompanied by professional musicians and an entertaining message all neatly packaged into a thirty-minute program that included some serious time dedicated to fundraising. I was twenty-two years old, my congregation numbered less than fifty, and our annual budget was less than $15,000.00. "Pastor, Rex Humbard really preached a great message this morning. Did you watch? And that daughter of his can really sing!" Without people and resources, how was I to compete?

But we have tried. In the past few decades churches have produced slicker bulletins and ever more dazzling PowerPoint or MediaShout presentations during worship or the sermon. We have tried to outdo each other for the coolest websites and most extravagant buildings. We have choreographed and scripted our services in a minute-by-minute format to pack as much energy and enthusiasm as possible into those sixty or ninety minutes on Sunday morning. As a pastor for nearly thirty years, I have witnessed the evolution and for the most part I have been a willing participant.

However, as the results of the Reveal survey bear witness, I have been forced to ask the question, "How is it working for us?" And to ask even more personally, "How is it working for me?" I remember my first attempts at using PowerPoint to illustrate my sermon and trying to coordinate the slides with the major points. It frustrated both me and my audience. Growing more proficient in the technology with use, I eventually would spend hours each week building a PowerPoint presentation to go along with my sermon, along with a published manuscript which was distributed to the congregation during all three morning services, and also posted to our website. I felt like I was doing a good job of "getting the Word out" and training my congregation. In the end, though, gnawing questions made me wonder.

If I could barely remember my sermon from the previous week, how could anyone else? So I began focusing more on application questions and next steps to go along with the sermon. Eventually, I prepared a weekly set of study questions and open-ended discussion starters to go along with each Sunday's message. I then encouraged our small group leaders to use these as the format for the study in their home groups the following week. While this was far more successful than simply preaching a message on Sunday morning with no accompanying visuals or follow-up, it still seemed "canned" to many people and sometimes missed the mark of where the people in the group were at that particular moment in time on their journey of faith.

As a pastor, not only did I utilize technology, but I also took a pro-grammatic, big business approach to the local church. Back in the 1990s, with a large church facility situated on twenty-four acres right on the main interstate halfway between Portland and Seattle, we were ideally located to serve as a regional church. And we were growing. My vision as the lead pastor encompassed reaching everyone possible in our geo-graphical region. More programs to reach children and families seemed to be the solution. So during the decade we continued to hire additional pastoral staff—eventually having a children's pastor, junior high/middle school pastor, high school/college pastor, singles pastor, seniors pastor, music/worship arts pastor, executive pastor, and a choir director. Mean-while we continued to grow within the baby boomer and builder genera-tions we were programmed to reach. In fact, when I assumed the lead pastor role in 1991, I was about thirty-five years old. Within a few years, the median age of the congregation became the same age as I was at the time. And it continued to grow older, right along with me! However we could not help but notice we were not reaching the growing population of twenty-somethings in our area. This also gnawed at me.

When I first went to the church, all of the pastoral staff marched out onto the platform at the appointed hour on Sunday morning—all dressed in formal suit and tie. The organ played, and the choir sang an anthem to begin the service—very traditional, and very polished. Even the way we served communion was orchestrated in a very precise order with ushers lining up like troops, moving on my command as I tried to figure out the complicated procedures and be sure I had properly folded the linens on the communion table. I am a detailed and orderly person, but even I was frustrated by the rules of engagement necessary to pull off a Sunday morning service.

So over the years we prayed, planned, and implemented changes. One subtle change involved moving from a very formal dress code to a more casual approach. This came about because one day a church member who worked as a mechanic brought a friend to church on a Sunday morning. Later that week, we talked about his friend's impressions. "Well, he generally liked the service, but said he thought you were wearing a $500 suit and wondered if he could really fit in here."

I had never paid $500 for a suit in my life, usually buying them on sale at J.C. Penney or another lower-end retailer. But I did not want the way I dressed to interfere with our outreach to the community, which is made up mainly of hardworking blue-collar individuals. Although the local market was changing, our county's historical economy was based upon the agriculture and forest industries—groups not known to have a fascination with *Project Runway*. But our church did not entirely reflect this community reality. For years we had been known as an upwardly mobile congregation serving an upper-middle-class, comparatively well-educated clientele.

Taking a cue from my mechanic friend, I used his story to convince our leadership team (it didn't really take much convincing) that we needed a more casual approach, including our dress code. This was around mid-1999, and we determined to make the change from Sunday morning "suits and ties only" on the first Sunday of 2000, Y2K fears aside. I had been reading John P. Cotter's book, *Leading Change*, and knew that we needed to create a sense of urgency and also give ample time to prepare people for this change. So for the next several months, I would make intentional comments about the fact that the first of next year, I would not be wearing a suit and tie every Sunday, presenting good reasons for the change.

So on that first Sunday of the new millennium, I stood before the mirror wearing a casual shirt and sweater, looked over at my wife and paraphrasing Esther from the Old Testament said, "If I perish, I perish!" Well, I didn't perish, but there were still people who continued to make comments about the change, thinking we were somehow compromising by doing away with long-held traditions. After all, most of us had been taught that Sunday was the Lord's Day, and you should reflect your very best on Sunday by "dressing up for the Lord." Frankly, I don't think the Lord is all that impressed by a suit and tie. However, many of the folks in the church continued to make comments when I did wear a suit on the rare Sunday, or for a funeral or wedding. "You really look like a pastor today!" they would say.

Another problem we faced was whether or not to build a new sanctuary. We could seat more than 500 people in the one we had, and the conventional wisdom about such matters agrees that if visitors sense the appearance of crowding, growth will be stifled. So we spent a few years talking to architects and discussing plans to build a sanctuary to seat 1,500 people—in a community of 1350 people (Napavine, Washington). But we were attracting people from all over the region, and were filling our sanctuary. Eventually we did build, and spent more than a million dollars to do so, which seemed like a lot of money to us at the time, but we did not build a new sanctuary. Instead, we built more meeting spaces that could be used for children and students, space that could be configured in a variety of ways. To accommodate growth, we chose to utilize the existing sanctuary for multiple services.

However, the change to a more casual dress code and adding building facilities did not change the reality that we were not reaching younger generations of adults. So in 2003 we made a strategic decision to add a third worship service in an attempt to reach that group. We did not want to change the substance of what we were doing on Sunday morning, only the style. The decision was made to place the new worship service during the same time slot as our traditional Sunday school program, because we believed that most adults would stay plugged into that and leave us plenty of room to grow the new service. We called the new service, "Day One" and it marked a significant change in style and environment with different lighting, a guitar-driven worship band, and an ambiance designed to reach a younger audience.

Part of our strategy involved marketing the early, 8:00 A.M. service to our senior adult population. We said, "If you have been attending church most of your life and love to sing songs you know by memory, then this service is for you." This group constituted the primary audience who attended the early service anyway, so it did not represent a significant change for them. We kept the basic format of our later, 10:45 A.M. service, with vibrant, more contemporary worship led by a worship team and a band, and including numbers by the choir or special groups. Leading up to these changes, I would often say (although it is not original with me), "Let's just give it a try. If it doesn't work, we can always go back to the way things weren't working before!"

I was very gratified by the fact that the new service format was an early success. I was surprised however, by the pushback from a number of people cross-generationally who voiced various complaints, from the loudness of the music to the fact some of the younger crowd wore inappropriate attire in church or sported too many tattoos or body-piercings. One woman was particularly upset that some of the young men in attendance wore their hats throughout the service. "Would you rather they were someplace else on Sunday morning?" I asked, which seemed like to me like a reasonable question in response to her complaints. But it failed to placate the traditionalists.

Two things stood out to me in our sometimes-successful attempts to re-define church, as we moved from a polished machine to a more organic and messy approach to reaching the people within our community whom Jesus died for. First, I did not anticipate the number of people who were actually quietly hoping for change and fully embraced what we were doing. The fact is, many of them probably would have moved on elsewhere if we had not made significant changes. This was illustrated by the fact that from the beginning our "Day One" service attracted a good number of representatives from the boomer generation, old rockers who loved the new guitar-driven music. Surprisingly, a number of seniors also attended, wanting to see what their grandchildren were up to, or in some cases, feeling that they could now invite their grandchildren to attend church with them.

The other surprise, which I already alluded to, was the fact that so many people were opposed to change of any kind. While I thought offering "something for everyone" would solve problems and answer objections, I thought differently after a few weeks of accusations from, "Are you just trying to draw a crowd so you can create a megachurch?" to "You are dividing the generations!" The accusations hurt, but also helped us keep evaluating the rationale for what we were doing; we wanted to be sure we were truly fulfilling our core values and mission as a church.

The fact is, we were trying to fulfill the mission of God, by reaching unreached "people groups" within our own community context. By the time I left the church to take the role I now have as a denominational executive, the church had grown to around 800 in regular attendance during the three Sunday morning services and we had more than 1500 adherents. That's not a megachurch by any means, but it is significant when you consider the largely rural community context, with approximately 12,000 people living within a five-mile radius.

In the years since leaving that pastorate, I have been speaking in a different church almost every Sunday. And I am more convinced than ever that postmoderns and younger generations are not nearly as fascinated with slick, polished programs and services as those of us who follow models of church created by members of the builder or boomer generation. This is even reflected in the way I preach today as opposed to five or six years ago. Today I rarely use PowerPoint or other forms of media, and I try to contextualize my message to my audience, conveying the truths of Scripture through stories and word pictures.

Organic spiritual formation is not a polished, linear process that can be easily reproduced with a curriculum or template that works everywhere. So much depends upon geography, community context, and generational differences. Even the climate makes a difference. I have visited

a number of large churches in Southern California that make use of out-
door spaces for everything from small group meeting places to baptis-
mal pools, bookstores or prayer stations. It seems to be working great for
them, but that particular strategy would never work for colder climes in
most of North America. Jesus interacted in different ways with different
people in different places to produce spiritual growth. When we allow
him to do the same with and through us, his light and love shine through
to produce authentic fruit, without the need for artificial polish.

FOR FURTHER PERSONAL OR GROUP STUDY

1. What are some aspects of a structured church service that
   could enhance spiritual growth? Is that the best place for
   growth to take place?

2. How would you describe your preference for a particular
   style of church—polished or organic? Why, and does it matter, in your opinion?

3. How can traditions be good things and/or helpful to spiritual
   growth? How might they hinder or even prevent spiritual
   growth?

4. What other environments outside of a traditional church
   building could promote spiritual growth? How have you
   seen this occur?

5. As people become more suspicious of organized religion,
   how might you connect those with Jesus who are open to
   spirituality?

CHAPTER THIRTEEN
Teamwork Makes Harvest Possible

Regardless of the type of farm, the overall operation rises and falls on the harvest. A successful mission or season of farming depends upon the harvest. Staying on mission means focusing on properly executing all of the steps necessary to bring in the harvest. Every farmer knows that if he fails to bring in the harvest, no matter how good he may have been in planting, weeding, or pest control, he has failed.

Although we seldom used the word, virtually everything we did on the farm involved teamwork. Family members, which included at times extended family members, worked together to accomplish tasks that would have been impossible for any one of us to do alone. From bringing in the hay, to building a barn, to cutting and wrapping meat or canning produce or hauling firewood, we worked together.

When there were really big projects to accomplish, such as building a bigger barn or building, we often worked with neighbors as well. Together, we toiled and everyone did his or her part to accomplish the goal. There existed no particular hierarchy, with middle-aged men working along-side teenagers or senior citizens, each doing what he or she could do best according to their own level of skill or expertise. Artisans with years of experience willingly and without cost patiently taught younger members of the team skills that would greatly enhance their lives with the expectation that they, in turn, would train another person down the road. Thus, healthy tradition and craftsmanship continued on in an organic fashion, without bureaucratic paperwork or organizational bylaws.

Jesus showed us how teams work. He never appointed a committee or chaired a board meeting, but he was the undisputed leader. He led by example and did not try to micromanage his disciples' activities. He empowered them to succeed and encouraged them when they failed and coached them when they needed to take the next steps in the journey.

TEAMS AND COMMUNITY

The Homestead Act of 1862 promised homesteaders on the American frontier a quarter section of land, 160 acres, if they agreed to build a home at least twelve by fourteen feet, and farm the land for five years. Because of the abundance of cheap land prior to this, many early settlers purchased at least a section of land, 640 acres or one square mile, from the government for $1 an acre.

These new residents of the frontier west were unaccustomed to dwelling on such large properties and did not fully realize the potential pitfalls of isolation. Thus, they often staked out and built their homes right in the middle of their property. When each of the farmers in the township did the same, it meant that every neighbor was at least a mile away from the nearest neighbor, even further if more than a section of land was owned. What this meant in a practical way was that neighbors soon discovered that they were too far away from one another. Particularly during times of emergency, and without telephone lines or any other means of communication, a mile away might as well have been fifty miles.

Recognizing the disadvantages of isolation, settlers began building closer to one another. The notion that one needed to be far away from the neighbors melted in the face of the urgent, pragmatic need to stick together for protection, mutual exchange of services, and socializing. This need for working together as a team was no more fully realized than in times of harvest.

HARVEST

Members of agricultural communities join together to bring in the harvest. This is a time-honored core value that recognizes the importance of teamwork and synergy, that the combined effort of the whole, working together, is greater than the sum of the parts working individually. Farmers were community organizers long before the term was popularized by politicians.

As a boy, I have fond memories of helping my elderly neighbor, Grandpa Plake, bring in his hay. I started when I was about ten years old, and continued to work with him until I graduated from high school. Although we were not related, everyone in our neighborhood called these dear folks Grandpa, or "Gramps" and Granny Plake.

"Now Donnie, I'll tell you what, Mr. Man, we've got to get all this hay baled and put up in the barn" he would say as he tried to start his ancient orange Allis Chalmers tractor. "I'll be needing it to feed the cows come winter."

Actually, his words were more of a wheeze than anything else, the result of a lifetime of smoking Camel cigarettes. Gramps was a skinny beanpole of a weathered old man, his face as wrinkled as the bark on an ancient oak. He would give you the shirt off his back if he thought you needed it, and I enjoyed helping him (although I sometimes wonder how much help I really was, because the eighty-pound bales weighed almost as much as I did when I began working with him). The sweat poured from our brows as we worked together to get the job done. There is no way I could have done the work by myself, especially at the age of ten. Gramps could never have done it alone either. I think I provided him the moral support and companionship that made it possible. Together, we always brought in the hay. Granny would fix us a big meal at lunch, and we would say grace, honoring the Lord for his provision and another year of harvest.

A harvest is always anticipated. No one plants a crop and expects it to fail. The investment is too great. The Bible uses the metaphor of fruit to describe intentionality. "Be fruitful, and multiply," God told Adam and Eve (Genesis 1:32). Jesus called us to "go, and bring forth fruit" (John 15:16). "The fruit of the Spirit" (Galatians 5:22) describes the qualities of maturation that result from organic growth.

When it comes to spiritual formation, we should expect to become fruitful followers of Jesus. At any given point in time, an organism is either dying, declining, living, growing, or thriving. The same is true for our spiritual growth. Where do you see yourself in that continuum? What would it take to change? How can you engage more fully in your own spiritual formation so you can expect to be a participant in the harvest? Perhaps you can begin by making a fuller commitment to obedience to God's Word. Eugene Peterson, translator of *The Message* version of the Bible, writes:

> At age 35 I bought running shoes and began enjoying the smooth rhythms of long-distance running. Soon I was competing in 10K races every month or so, and then a marathon once a year. By then I was subscribing to and reading three running magazines! Then I pulled a muscle and couldn't run for a couple of months. Those magazines were still all over the house, but I never opened one. The moment I resumed running, though, I started reading again.
>
> That's when I realized that my reading was an extension of something I was a part of. I was reading for companionship and affirmation of the experience of running. I learned a few things along the way, but mostly it was to deepen my world of running. If I wasn't running, there was nothing to deepen.The parallel with reading Scripture is striking. If I'm not living in active response to the living God, reading about his creation/salvation/holiness won't hold my interest for long. The most important question isn't "What does this mean," but "What can I obey?" Simple obedience will open up our lives to a text more quickly than any number of Bible studies, dictionaries, and concordances.[1]

Obedience to Jesus Christ opens the door for growth, and obedience often means working to bring in the harvest. It is understood that proper nourishment, cultivation, and environment are all necessary for sustained growth at every stage of development. Faith, life, and community lead to fruit, the organic result for harvest. When this is not the case, or when growth is stunted, it's time to get back to basics. The writer of Hebrews spoke to this issue:

In fact, though by this time you ought to be teachers, you need someone to teach you the elementary truths of God's word all over again. You need milk, not solid food! Anyone who lives on milk, being still an infant, is not acquainted with the teaching about righteousness. But solid food is for the mature, who by constant use have trained themselves to distinguish good from evil. (Hebrews 5:12–14)

Spiritual formation and the resulting harvest have a lot to do with sowing and reaping. If you don't invest much on the sowing end of things, you won't reap much of a harvest. But even a small investment can reap great dividends if we invest in the right things.

Granny and Gramps, mentioned earlier, knew the value of investment in things that truly matter. While you'd never have known it by looking at their humble home and surroundings, they were storing up eternal treasures by investing in people. They raised many of their own grandchildren whose parents had died, and their kindness extended beyond their family to neighbors and even strangers who were welcomed to partake of Granny's meals.

Granny and Gramps were a team during nearly seventy years of marriage, up until the end of their lives. Everyone thought that Gramps would go first, even though he eventually gave up his smoking habit. But somewhat surprisingly, the spry and seemingly healthy Granny ended up in the hospital and then an extended-care facility because of congestive heart failure. I visited and prayed with them often, and was there the day Granny went to heaven. Grief-stricken Gramps went home and the next morning a grandson found him slumped over in a chair with a smile on his face. Their separation had not been long, as both were reunited at the feet of their Savior. At their combined memorial service, hundreds of relatives, friends, and neighbors paid tribute to this humble couple who teamed up to make a difference in the lives of others.

Who can measure the value and eventual harvest of seeds planted in faith? On September 26, 1940, Perry Hayden began an experiment that lasted for six years. He based his research on Jesus' words in John 12:24,

"The truth is, a kernel of wheat must be planted in the soil. Unless it dies it will be alone—a single seed. But its death will produce many new kernels—a plentiful harvest of new lives" (NKJV).

Working the soil in a plot of ground four by eight feet, Perry planted a cubic inch of wheat, 360 kernels, in 12 little rows. The next year brought a harvest of 18,000 kernels (50 cubic inches), fifty times the amount of wheat sowed. A tithe of that first crop was given to the pastor of the local Friends church. The remaining 90 percent was planted as a basis for next year's crop.

This process continued for six years. In spite of bad weather—and always giving away ten percent of the crop—each year a greater amount was harvested. By the time the experiment ended in 1946, the plot had grown from four by eight feet to nearly 2,700 acres. Henry Ford got interested in the project and a number of companies (including Ford) furnished supplies, tractors, and harvesting equipment. In the final year, 360 kernels of grain had grown to more than 72,150 bushels of wheat harvested by 276 farmers involved in the project. Compared to the single cubic inch of grain planted the first year, this represented a multiplication factor of 155,152,803. The crop that year was made into cereal by the Ralston Purina Company and distributed overseas for famine relief by the Friends Service Committee.[2]

JESUS, WORSHIP, AND THE HARVEST

Most Christians these days would agree with Rick Warren's assertion in *The Purpose Driven Life* that God has created us for the purposes of worship, fellowship, discipleship, evangelism, and service. I believe it can serve as a framework for organic spiritual formation in the context of faith, life, and community. However, many people associate the purposes of God with an event, or series of events, rather than a lifestyle.

Worship is not an event. In fact, Jesus showed us that worship and harvest are connected. Let me explain by asking a few questions:

- Is *where* we worship significant?
- Is *when* we worship significant?
- Is *how* we worship significant?

John chapter four contains the story of Jesus and the Samaritan woman at the well. During this brief encounter with a sinful woman, we catch a glimpse of how Jesus interacted with people different from himself, the importance of coming to grips with our own sinfulness, and the need for true worship.

Now he had to go through Samaria. So he came to a town in Samaria called Sychar, near the plot of ground Jacob had given to his son Joseph. Jacob's well was there, and Jesus, tired as he was from the journey, sat down by the well. It was about the sixth hour.

When a Samaritan woman came to draw water, Jesus said to her, "Will you give me a drink?" (His disciples had gone into the town to buy food.)The Samaritan woman said to him, "You are a Jew and I am a Samaritan woman. How can you ask me for a drink?" (For Jews do not associate with Samaritans.)

Jesus answered her, "If you knew the gift of God and who it is that asks you for a drink, you would have asked him and he would have given you living water."

"Sir," the woman said, "you have nothing to draw with and the well is deep. Where can you get this living water? Are you greater than our father Jacob, who gave us the well and drank from it himself, as did also his sons and his flocks and herds?"

Jesus answered, "Everyone who drinks this water will be thirsty again, but whoever drinks the water I give him will never thirst. Indeed, the water I give him will become in him a spring of water welling up to eternal life."

The woman said to him, "Sir, give me this water so that I won't get thirsty and have to keep coming here to draw water."

He told her, "Go, call your husband and come back."

"I have no husband," she replied.

Jesus said to her, "You are right when you say you have no husband. The fact is, you have had five husbands, and the man you now have is not your husband. What you have just said is quite true."

"Sir," the woman said, "I can see that you are a prophet. Our fathers worshiped on this mountain, but you Jews claim that the place where we must worship is in Jerusalem."

Jesus declared, "Believe me, woman, a time is coming when you will worship the Father neither on this mountain nor in Jerusalem. You Samaritans worship what you do not know; we worship what we do know, for salvation is from the Jews. Yet a time is coming and has now come when the true worshipers will worship the Father in spirit and truth, for they are the kind of worshipers the Father seeks. God is spirit, and his worshipers must worship in spirit and in truth."

The woman said, "I know that Messiah" (called Christ) "is coming. When he comes, he will explain everything to us."

Then Jesus declared, "I who speak to you am he."

Just then his disciples returned and were surprised to find him talking with a woman. But no one asked, "What do you want?" or "Why are you talking with her?"

Then, leaving her water jar, the woman went back to the town and said to the people, "Come, see a man who told me everything I ever did. Could this be the Christ?" (John 4:4–29)

This is an intriguing story and one with many applications. Although most Jews would have nothing to do with the Samaritans and would go out of their way to avoid their territory, Jesus specifically journeyed there. John 4:4 indicates he was compelled to travel through Samaria, even though it was not the direct route to where he was going. The New Testament records a number of instances where Jesus ministered to Samaritans. And we should never forget that Jesus told the story of the Good Samaritan (see Luke 10:30–37).

The Samaritans were a mixed race, and came about as a result of the Assyrian captivity of the ten northern tribes of Israel in 727 B.C. When the enemies of Jesus wanted to call him an insulting name in John 8:48, they called him a Samaritan!

Samaritans were not accepted by the Jews. Yet the Samaritans had much in common with them, and patterned their worship after the Jews.

However, they also mixed in other elements of pagan religion, thus making the Samaritan religion distinctive and an abomination to the Jews. 2 Kings 17:33 describes Samaritan worship: "They worshipped the Lord, but they also served their own gods in accordance with the customs of the nations from which they had been brought."

Near Sychar was Mount Gerizim (2849 feet tall). The Samaritans built a temple there to rival the temple in Jerusalem. They believed Mount Gerizim was Mount Moriah. The Hasmonean ruler John Hyrcanus destroyed the Samaritan temple in 113 B.C. So during the time of Christ, the ruins of this Samaritan temple would have been clearly visible as Jesus talked with the woman at the well.

As Jesus talked with the woman about her life and the condition of her soul, she tried to distract him through a discussion about geography and worship. Her question was very relevant to us, because even today people associate worship with a place more than they do with a person. How many times have you heard the phrase "a house of worship?" Is where we worship important?

Jerusalem, and particularly the temple mount (Mount Moriah) and Mount Zion, were essential locations for worship to the Jew. Both the Jews and Samaritans were very concerned about and attracted to holy sites. Today this is a huge issue in the ongoing conflict in the Middle East, particularly as it relates to Jerusalem. Both the Jews and the Palestinians claim the temple mount and Jerusalem as their holy city. Both the Jews and the Muslims are willing to die defending their holy sites from desecration.

Today's bitter wrath between the Jews and Palestinians over holy sites is similar to the animosity between the Jews and Samaritans in Jesus' day. And much of that bitterness and misunderstanding had to do with the location of worship.

Many people, when they think about religion, think about a specific place. Some of the greatest architectural wonders in history have been churches or places of worship. For the Jews, the place of worship is Jerusalem. For Muslims, it is Mecca. For Hindus, it is a dip in the Ganges River. For Roman Catholics, it is Rome. For Mormons, it is Salt Lake City. But true worship transcends any particular geographical place.

Church buildings, crucifixes, beads, or religious icons may be beautiful to behold, but they are not objects worthy of worship. They merely symbolize the greatness and majesty of God. In the early church, worship services were first conducted in private houses. Possibly for a time the first Christians worshipped in the synagogues as well as private homes. Some scholars believe the Jewish Christians would go to the synagogues on Saturday and to their own meeting on Sunday.

Over the course of time, churches began to be built, as congregations grew too large to meet in individual homes. There is nothing wrong with church buildings, or with meeting in them. But we must always remember that they are just buildings. Although they may be dedicated to God, he doesn't live there—he lives in the hearts of his people!

True worship results in a lifestyle that honors God, not religious traditions. Jesus told this woman, "You Samaritans worship what you do not know; we worship what we do know, for salvation is from the Jews. Yet a time is coming and has now come when the true worshipers will worship the Father in spirit and truth" (John 4:22–23a).

The woman at the well was like many people, unwilling to really come to terms with her own sinfulness. Instead, she diverted her attention to religious questions and arguments about traditions and diversity, questions clothed in a garment of ambiguity. Jesus got to the heart of her issue, her sinful heart and lifestyle. You cannot worship God until you really know him and come into right relationship with him. As Jesus said, many people are ignorant about worship. They simply don't understand it, so they "worship what they do not know."

From the history of the 1980s you might read about or even remember the Baghwan Shree Rajhneesh who drove Rolls Royces around his compound near Antelope, Oregon. My friend, Cap Marks, traveled there at the time to see about purchasing some surplus equipment from them.

While there, he watched hundreds of devoted followers lift their hands and praise, sing and dance around the Baghwan. Cap had an opportunity to talk with some of the Rajhneeshees, as they were called, and asked them, "Why do you worship the Baghwan?"

Their response shocked him. "Oh, we don't worship the Baghwan," they said. "We worship worship."

Today, the Baghwan is dead, the Rajneeshees have disbanded, and their huge compound in Central Oregon is a Young Life Camp! But that statement, "We worship worship" has always haunted me as a reflection of the longing in every heart for something to worship. When a religious person has not learned how to biblically worship God through the Lord Jesus Christ, idolatry is the result.

The Apostle Paul encountered a similar situation when he visited Athens. After viewing their many idols and seeing one even dedicated to, "the unknown god," Paul showed them how they could know him (Acts 17:21–33) through Jesus Christ. He also provided us some good insight into worship when he said, it is through God that, "we live, and breathe and have our being" (v. 28).

God wants us to worship him through a lifestyle that honors him. Paul wrote in Colossians 3:17, "And whatever you do in word or deed, do all in the name of the Lord Jesus, giving thanks to God the Father through Him" (NKJV). For the Christ-follower, this is the basis for our lifestyle and our worship. We should live in such a way that everything we do is done for the Lord as an act of worship—whether at home, at work, or at play. When we do, spiritual formation will result, organically, because our focus will be upon Jesus, the root of our faith.

Is when we worship important? Jesus said "now is the time" for us to worship! The Jewish Sabbath was quickly replaced by the first day of the week as the time for weekly public worship (see Acts 20:7; 1 Corinthians 16:2); it was called the Lord's Day (see Revelation 1:10). This was the occasion for celebration of the resurrection of Jesus, since he rose from the dead on the first day of the week (see Mark 16:2).

Psalm 34 is one of my favorites. It instructs us to worship the Lord at all times. "I will bless the Lord at all times: his praise shall continually be in my mouth. My soul shall make her boast in the Lord: the humble shall hear thereof, and be glad. O magnify the Lord with me, and let us exalt his name together" (Psalm 34, 1–3, KJV).

Is how we worship important? Jesus said the Father is seeking people who would worship him in spirit and in truth. It is not enough to worship in ways that we are comfortable with or that seem right to us. Our worship must come from a walk with Jesus Christ, led by the Holy Spirit. In talking about worship as a lifestyle, Paul wrote, "If we live in the Spirit, let us also walk in the Spirit" (Galatians 5:25, NKJV). A passionate walk with the Lord will result in a worshipful walk.

At the time of Christ, the Jews worshipped according to the truth of the Scriptures. The Samaritans worshipped with a spirit of worship, but using the wrong methods and holding to their own traditions instead of Scripture. Thus, Jesus was saying we were to balance our worship with both the leading of the Holy Spirit and the truth of the Scriptures. The Spirit without the truth can become mere emotionalism. The truth without the Spirit can bring dryness and death. Both are needed to bring life.

Details about the worship procedures of the early Christians in the New Testament times are not given a lot of emphasis in Scripture, but things like prayer, preaching, teaching, giving, communion, praise, and music are mentioned. These elements must have been regularly included in Christian worship since the first millennium and should be reflected in each believer's daily lifestyle. Regardless of the place, time, or elements of our worship—all of our worship should be in spirit and in truth. Worship is the continuous act of a believer passionately in love with Jesus, walking in the strength and power of the Holy Spirit and joyfully giving praise to God through all that he is and all that he does. Remember, worship is a lifestyle, not an event.

When the disciples returned and found Jesus speaking to this woman, it must have generated a lot of questions for them. Yet they kept their silence. Perhaps they missed an opportunity to learn, because we learn organically by asking questions. However, Jesus quickly got to the heart of the matter by responding to their unasked questions when they urged him to eat:

> Meanwhile his disciples urged him, "Rabbi, eat something."
> But he said to them, "I have food to eat that you know nothing about."

Then his disciples said to each other, "Could someone have brought him food?"

"My food," said Jesus, "is to do the will of him who sent me and to finish his work. Do you not say, 'Four months more and then the harvest?' I tell you, open your eyes and look at the fields! They are ripe for harvest. Even now the reaper draws his wages, even now he harvests the crop for eternal life, so that the sower and the reaper may be glad together. Thus the saying 'One sows and another reaps' is true. I sent you to reap what you have not worked for. Others have done the hard work, and you have reaped the benefits of their labor." (John 4:31–38)

Twenty-first century disciples of Jesus can take courage from the fact that even when Jesus' disciples were with him up close and personal, they often did not truly comprehend the spiritual dimensions of what he was doing. Sometimes the best thing we can do is listen and learn. Their concern was about physical matters, such as having lunch, and Jesus was concerned about a spiritual harvest.

We learn from this final Bible story in our conversation about organic spiritual formation that the mission of God is accomplished best by recognizing the opportunities that come our way to engage people in meaningful conversation. Even though culturally or ethnically different than us, as was the woman at the well, we can look for open windows of opportunity.

Immediately after this encounter with the woman, Jesus' pointed lesson had to do with the harvest. Spiritual food is more important than physical food. The cure for spiritual blindness is to open our eyes to the world as Jesus sees the world. The harvest is now. Corrie ten Boom once said, "The measure of a life is not its duration, but its donation." Even today, the opportunities exist at every watering hole or place that people gather to socialize for a meaningful exchange, showing the Lord's love. As we do, we sow seeds that may one day result in a harvest. And as we sow, we grow organically.

THE FUTURE

I have intentionally not attempted to lay out a linear, step-by-step process for spiritual growth. Nor do I believe it requires an either/or approach between organic and programmatic processes. In fact, an artificial bifurcation of the sacred and the secular is one of the reasons why spiritual growth is often ignored in the marketplace of life, and relegated to what occurs at "church."

I have attempted to show how the spiritual life must intersect with all of life in a simple and organic fashion. Even home-schooling advocates realize that children typically require some structure, classroom, or curriculum to foster learning. In the same way, both intentional structures and organic processes through faith, life, and community nurture spiritual growth both at home and through the church.

In *Christianity Today* Richard Foster shared his "spiritual formation agenda" for the next thirty years. He lists heart work, "fellowship gathering power," and cultural renewal as the key ingredients for the ongoing work of spiritual formation.

"Heart work" describes the importance of taking individual responsibility to grow as a disciple. Heart work focuses on introspection, reflection, and meditation. External actions are never the center of attention, as Foster believes external action follows the essence of who we are on the inside. This perfectly correlates with the faith and life components of organic spiritual formation.

"Fellowship gathering power" describes Foster's priority of congregational renewal. He notes the lack of vitality within the organized church and cites a number of causes, to include an overall consumer mentality, which includes entertainment as a substitute for worship and spirituality. He sees a new focus on spiritual formation within a congregational context an emerging re-formation of the church. Again, the principles of organic spiritual formation fit well within the context of the church as community.

Foster lists cultural renewal as the final leg of his three-legged vision for taking spiritual formation to the next level over the next generation. He affirms the importance of allowing God to pluck the world out of our hearts, as we lose the attachment to position, prominence, or power. We are then better equipped in the power of the Spirit to engage the world as we embrace the mission of God. Citing St. Patrick, Francis of Asisi, Wilberforce, and Mother Teresa as examples, he makes a good case for organically transforming the church organizationally into a missional force within its community context.[3]

I hope to have planted some seeds of curiosity that will inspire you to reflect further on your own spiritual growth, and dig deep in the soil of your own soul to provide fertile ground for growth. In the next chapter and the afterword, I want to help clarify the importance of understanding your mission, and the mission of the church in growing disciples. Confusion about the mission makes spiritual formation seem more like wandering through a confusing maze than a joyful journey of growth.

FOR FURTHER PERSONAL OR GROUP STUDY

1. Describe the best team you have ever been a part of. What made it a good experience? What were some of the challenges? How did the leader impact the rest of the team?

2. What comes to mind when you think about harvest in terms of spirituality?

3. In your opinion, what are the outcomes of spiritual maturity?

4. "Spiritual formation and the resulting harvest have a lot to do with sowing and reaping." What is your church or spiritual community doing to sow seed in preparation for a harvest?

5. What do you think the church would look like if people actually worked together as a team or teams toward a common mission and purpose?

6. What did you learn about worship and spiritual growth from the story of the Samaritan woman?

7. How would you describe your own personal attitude about or practice of worship?

CHAPTER FOURTEEN

Mission Clarification

It seemed like such a good idea at the time. It turned out to be one of the biggest mistakes I ever made. Although I was far from being an experienced leader back then, it also turned out to be a defining moment in my life that helped shape my thinking about leadership and staying true to mission.

As a college student in 1975 I worked the swing shift in a Eugene, Oregon sawmill. I took my place at the bottom of the food chain, in a system of position and power based upon seniority and hierarchy. The guys referred to me as the "cleanup boy," a belittling label that I endured because I earned a whopping $4.50 an hour, while the minimum wage in 1975 hovered a little over $2.00 an hour. My job required me to clean the mechanic's shop and equipment. Having grown up on a farm, I was used to cleaning up after livestock, so I figured this could not be much different. Besides, the smell of sawdust beats the aroma of manure any day.

In addition, I knew how to operate tractors and machinery. Working in the sawmill expanded my operating portfolio as I drove forklifts of all sizes, log trucks, and assorted heavy equipment for the purpose of combatting their grease and grime with a steam cleaner. The work was dirty, noisy, physical, and sometimes monotonous. I took my responsibility seriously and made it my mission to keep everything as clean as possible. At times that seemed like a never-ending task because the mechanics and various machinists working in the shop knew how to make a mess, and never cleaned up after themselves.

One night I completed my regular tasks, and set to work organizing and cleaning up one particular storage area of the machine shop. A large pile of old metal parts seemed to be taking up a lot of space, gathering dirt, and making it difficult to keep the area clean. My muscles ached as I hauled the heavy metal components out to the dumpster where they would soon be deported as scrap. Looking over the newly cleaned up area, I beamed with a sense of pride in my work, believing the foreman would be pleased with my initiative and hard work when he arrived in the morning.

When I got to work the next afternoon around 3:00 P.M., I was not surprised when one of the mechanics told me the foreman wanted to see me right away. I could barely contain my enthusiasm at the prospect of a word of commendation, or maybe even a raise, promotion, or bonus. Upon arrival, the sour look on the foreman's face soon took the wind out of my sails. "What did you think you were doing by hauling all those parts out to the dumpster last night?" he boomed.

"Well, I just got tired of cleaning up around that mess, so I thought I would get rid of all that junk," I stammered.

"That pile of junk, as you called it, contained parts necessary to keep this sawmill in operation in case of a breakdown. You threw away about $20,000.00 worth of parts last night! It's a good thing one of the mechanics noticed after you left last night, and lugged everything back in. If those parts had still been in that dumpster when it got hauled off this morning, you would be fired right now!"

Luckily, he was a Christian man and he knew I was a theology student, so he had mercy on me. Even though I did not lose my job, my mind reeled at the implications of my good intentions gone awry. Using my wages at $4.50 an hour, it would have taken me nearly five thousand hours to pay for my mistake. Twenty thousand dollars was a lot of money back in 1975, when you could buy a nice home for not much more than that in our area.

I thought I knew my mission, to clean up my part of the mill. But that particular evening I suffered from mission confusion, thinking that I was doing a good thing, while I was actually destroying the contingency plan for operation of the sawmill. The conversation with the foreman provided clarification. After that, I left the big decisions to the foreman, and asked before tackling a project that seemed like a good idea to me at the time.

The bigger mission of the sawmill, of course, did not center upon my role, as important as it might have seemed to me. The bigger mission involved keeping the entire organization operating efficiently so lumber could be produced, creating the raw materials for construction, building homes and industry. Keeping the larger mission in perspective requires perspective. Without that perspective, a cleanup boy might think his mission is just to clean up messes left by his fellow workers, and fail to realize that he is actually helping to make it possible for houses to be built, and for the local economy to flourish.

Without a view of the bigger picture, it is possible to lose sight of your purpose and true mission. In the same way, the custodian of a church might view his job as only cleaning rooms, picking up trash, or vacuuming the carpet. Yet in light of the bigger mission of the church, he could be an integral component in helping guests feel welcome in a clean and inviting environment, thus facilitating an openness to receive Christ.

KNOW THE MISSION, FIND THE FULCRUM

Understanding and executing the mission of the church is the fulcrum that leverages every potential component of organic spiritual formation into a tool of discipleship to build God's kingdom. Knowing the mission of God provides us with the vision to see fully developed disciples of Christ stemming from the raw material of human frailty.

Jesus saw potential in twelve men that others did not see. Beyond their rough exterior, he saw the construction materials necessary to build up his infant church. In the physical strength of these working men, he recognized the ability to endure struggles and pain in service to God. From their emotional outbursts and opinions he saw passionate hearts that could persuade men and change the world. He modeled God to them, and infused their hearts, minds, and physical strength with His Spirit, thus providing the fulcrum to leverage their maximum effectiveness.

Yet among Christians today, even among experienced church leaders, mission confusion abounds. Some believe the mission of the church is tradition, to preserve their particular doctrinal statement or denominational affiliation. Others believe their mission revolves around numbers, maintaining and exceeding metrics for buildings or budgets. Still others view their mission as relevance, and they expand programs, technology, and ministries to an ever-widening and diverse audience. Some point toward churches that experience explosive growth as they aim at the constantly moving target of popular culture. There are always those who believe the church's mission finds its best expression through social justice, or community organization and development. Then there are those who believe the church is all about worship, as they define it. And many are the churches that believe their mission to be the defense of truth, or their version of it, at any cost.

Please indulge me as I invite you to peruse the following mission statements or slogans, gleaned from a few minutes surfing the internet for church websites. It seems a bit lengthy, yet it illustrates the point. Feel free to pass quickly through the bulleted points to the text below. While there are several familiar themes, I think you will agree no actual consensus appears to exist amid quite a bit of confusion:

- *Our church is called to proclaim the Gospel of Christ and the beliefs of the evangelical Christian faith, to maintain the worship of God, and to inspire in all persons a love for Christ, a passion for righteousness, and a consciousness of their duties to God and their fellow human beings.*

- *Love God. Love others. Serve the world.*

- *Developing fully devoted followers of Christ.*

- *Our mission is to sow "the Seed of Hope," Jesus Christ, in the hearts of many here and to the ends of the earth. Our context is the emerging post-modern culture. Post-moderns have rejected the "trinity" of modernism: reason, nature and progress-and the church that is built on it. Lacking a metanarrative, post-moderns turn to a sort of primitive tribalism, or bury their pain in technology or consumerism.*

- *Our mission is to carry the gospel, the sacraments, and God's love and fellowship to the unchurched, the alienated, and the excommunicated (the church's homeless).*

- *Reaching out to the World ... Preaching to the Unsaved ... Teaching the Saved to Serve.*

- *To yield to the wind of the Holy Spirit blowing through our midst, allowing it to change us into the image of Christ, thus making us the loving people God would have us to be.*

- *Christian, in our beliefs ... Methodist, in our approach ... Episcopal, in our organization.*

- *We strive to be an "open-door" church, actively reaching out and welcoming all persons. A Great Place For Your Family!*

- *First Church especially focuses upon those who are seeking a "new beginning," and those who want to become more "Christ-like," and want to learn more about living a "holy life," and for those who are yearning to grow in "love and compassion," and the building of "family relationships."*

- *Where faith and adventure meet!*

- *To preach the gospel of Jesus Christ and to meet human needs in His name without discrimination.*

- *To teach, preach, and baptize all who will heed "The Word."*

- *To courageously represent the kingdom of God through witness, discipleship and service to others.*

- *To worship God as we evangelize the world, and provide a place of fellowship to equip the believer for service to God and man.*

- *The goal of our mission is to introduce all who can be reached to our precious Lord Jesus, whose return to rapture His Church is so imminent.*

- *To increase our love for God and to help meet the needs of humankind by "Loving God with all our heart, with all our*

soul, and with all our mind, and to love our neighbor as
ourselves."

- We are a church that is committed to Christ and his Word.

- We are a church where we "Exalt the Savior," "Evangelize the
Sinner"and "Equip the Saint."

- To make Christ known to the world through a loving, growing,
giving and serving group of committed people who are connected in small groups.

- "The Word of God is our focus."

- A church that strives to be a beacon of light in our community

- The Church that understands that people don't care about
how much you know, until they know how much you care

- Our purpose here is to reach as many people with the good
news of Jesus Christ as possible through: Relevant and challenging messages from our pastor—An exciting atmosphere of
praise and worship during our services.

- We are a full Gospel church that believes everything the Bible
states. We believe that Jesus Christ is the Son of God. We preach
and teach the truth. We have the desire to see souls saved.

- Our mission is to save, educate and liberate humanity for
Jesus the Christ by sharing the Gospel Message, teaching the
Bible, and living in the power of the Holy Spirit.

- Where everybody is somebody and Jesus is Lord.

From the pleasantly simple to the painfully complex, churches struggle
to define their mission. How do you synthesize twenty-seven New Testament books containing thousands of verses into a simple mission statement,
proclaiming the main thing? With the variety of churches and Christian
organizations, is it possible to define the mission of the church organically?

It may be helpful for us to take another look at the organic motif. The
Oxford English Dictionary defines organic as, "relating to, or derived from

living matter." The word comes from the Greek word, *organikos*, "relating to a tool or instrument." "Organize" and "organization" also stem from the same root word. Although *organikos* is not found in the New Testament, we do find familiar themes of building, tools, and workmanship. Something organic derives from something living. Paul expresses our connection to Christ, "For we are God's workmanship, created in Christ Jesus to do good works, which God prepared in advance for us to do" (Ephesians 2:10) The Greek word for workmanship, poiema, conveys the idea of craftsmanship, something organically fabricated, like linen cloth.

Perhaps the best mission statement for the church is an extrapolation of the one Jesus provided just before his ascension. Long known as "The Great Commission," the words of Matthew 28:18–20 indicate our co-mission with Christ—providing explanation and substance for the "good works" Paul mentioned that "God prepared in advance for us to do" (Ephesians 2:10):

> Then Jesus came to them and said, "All authority in heaven and on earth has been given to me. Therefore go and make disciples of all nations, baptizing them in the name of the Father and of the Son and of the Holy Spirit, and teaching them to obey everything I have commanded you. And surely I am with you always, to the very end of the age." (Matthew 28:18–20)

There is nothing new here; expositors wrestle with this text and preachers expound on its urgency on a regular basis, as they have done for all the centuries since Jesus first uttered the words. Yet the profound simplicity of these words conveys an uncomplicated, organic message for continuation of the church, our true mission for organic growth, coming directly from the living Head of the church.

Personally, I shy away from simplistic approaches and have done so throughout this book. Our modern and post-modern tendencies to discover linear solutions and offer a one-size-fits-all, "how-to" solution cannot find basis in Scripture. So we try to make texts say what we want them to say, in order to come up with a program or process for disciple-making. Yet I cannot escape the fact that Jesus' organic commission can provide a steady and sturdy skeleton upon which our spiritual formation depends. We all look different on the outside, but we all look very similar within. That is a picture of the church in our diversity, yet having a structure framed by Christ himself. For those of you looking for an outline, here it is, alliteration and all:

EMPOWERMENT (VERSE 18)

Notice the words of Jesus: "all authority ... therefore go...." We cannot begin to think about accomplishing God's mission without God's authorization and power. Just as the disciples needed the Upper Room experience, so we need the empowerment of the Holy Spirit to actively engage our culture, touch people, and be the church Jesus desires us to be. What could be more organic than a connection to the source of life?

EVANGELISM (VERSE 19)

"Make disciples, baptizing them ..." The same Holy Spirit that compelled the 120 disciples to move from the Upper Room to the streets invites us to move from our safe inner circles to where the people live in our context. This involves proclaiming the Gospel, the evangel, the good news—using both words and deeds. At various times the church has turned the good news into either an argument, a political profile, a creed to recite, or a polemic for a particular theological perspective. The simple truth remains that the Gospel is best conveyed as good news, in a personal conversation between two or more real people. Encountering people and building relationships with them is natural, not staged or forced. The early church grew, not because of programs, or crusades, or organizational skills. It grew because it was organic.

EDUCATION (VERSE 20A)

"Teaching them to obey ..." Notice the emphatic use of the strong words by Jesus: "obey" and "command." There is nothing prescribed or enforced about the method of teaching or style of ministry, but we are expected to educate others. How did people learn at the time of Christ? They learned by watching and listening. A disciple or learner was an apprentice, in close relationship with a mentor. There are those who will point to the Greek word *didasko* ("teaching" in verse 20a) to indicate a particular didactic style of teaching. However, it is clear that Jesus used a variety of methods to teach, based upon the need for information and condition of the learner. We have an obligation to teach, and content is more important than the style of delivery. The very task of educating all types of people in all settings with the most important message requires a more fluid, organic approach.

EXPERIENCE (VERSE 20B)

"Surely I am with you always ..." The continued presence of God within the community of believers and in the lives of individual believers may provide the very best antidote to skeptical or apathetic individual objections to faith in Christ. Cerebral protestations to the Gospel or even toward the idea of theism find themselves usurped by personal experience. When the church recognizes that part of our mission involves taking Jesus with us into the marketplaces and private spaces of our lives, we will influence others toward faith in him. People took note of the early believers and recognized that they had been with Jesus (see Acts 4:13). They had an experience with a living Savior through the power of the Holy Spirit that changed their lives.

Although I have tried to avoid formulaic approaches, my years of preaching have taught me that some people do remember and apply things better when we provide simple, clear, and concise messages. For what it might be worth to you, here is another approach I sometimes use to illustrate the same basic points above to convey the mission of The Great Commission:

Empowerment: Going on the mission.

Evangelism: Showing Jesus to others.

Education: Growing disciples.

Experience: Knowing that Jesus will never leave us.

The writer of Hebrews tells us that, "without faith it is impossible to please God, because anyone who comes to him must believe that he exists and that he rewards those who earnestly seek him" (Hebrews 11:6).

How could a return to these simple organic concepts Jesus so clearly explained help us reach into the lives of people who otherwise will persist in their unbelief? What if we truly loved the world as much as God does, and edited our mission statements in light of these truths? What if we examined our personal mission in the same light? We may discover that our core values and mission change when we learn the true value of those things we might ordinarily throw away.

Every disciple can access the basic components of faith, life, and community as they get on mission and write the personal story of their own unique faith journey with Jesus. Those vibrant stories will provide the next chapter in the history of the church. As John wrote about our Savior, "Jesus did many other things as well. If every one of them were written down, I suppose that even the whole world would not have room for the books that would be written" (John 21:25).

FOR FURTHER PERSONAL OR GROUP STUDY

1. How would you describe your mission in life?

2. If you have never before written out a mission statement or life purpose statement, why not explore the topic on the internet and do so? If you have done so in the past, why not review it and evaluate how it is working for you?

3. What did you think while reading through the various church mission statements? Is it important that there be alignment between a church's mission statement or core values and their actual practices?

4. Can you clearly define the mission of your own local church or community of faith? How does your church include discipleship its mission, core values, or purpose?

5. What is Jesus' Great Commission asking us to do, or, more specifically, what is He asking you to do?

6. What do you think about the idea of using the terms going, showing, growing, and knowing to illustrate the Great Commission?

7. What did you learn by reading this book? What did you like and find useful, and what wasn't?

8. How might you use what you learned by reading this book to become a more fully developed follower of Jesus and/or share that with others?

Afterword

A pastor friend of mine read the draft manuscript of this book. "What did you think of it?" I asked.

"I kept looking for the chapter called, How to Grow Spiritually in Three or Four Easy Steps," he replied. "And when I got to the end, I was glad you did not take that approach, because we have tried to create formulas for spiritual formation, and they simply do not work. The process is more complicated and organic than a linear step-by-step, one-size-fits-all program provides. We seem to promise that a lot, but don't have a method to deliver."

If you have stayed with me up to this point, perhaps you agree with my pastor friend. Then again, maybe you do not. Neither he nor I believe spiritual growth is an either/or process between organic and programs. It is decidedly both/and: both intentional and unintentional, both inside and outside the traditional walls of the church, both simple and complex. In any event, I have only begun to scratch the surface of the topic of growing disciples organically, or what I call organic spiritual formation. The Gospels alone contain enough material for a whole series of books exploring the subjects of faith, life, and community through the lens of organic growth.

I hope this book has whetted your appetite. And I hope you have begun the journey of faith in Jesus Christ and will follow where He leads you. As my friend, Pastor Wayne Cordeiro, has said in the title of a recent book, what we need is *Jesus, Pure and Simple*. Beyond that, we all need mentors, friends, coaches, pastors and the other elements and environments I've described to become a fully developed follower of Jesus.

The Holy Spirit works with us each in individual ways, organically and purposely forming us to become more like Jesus. It all begins with a seed of faith, and grows from there. I have tried to show how faith can intersect with every part of your life and shared numerous examples from my own life story and experiences of faith, life, and community. I will end with another story.

In the summer of 2002, my 85-year-old mother became critically ill and spent a number of days in the critical care unit of their local hospital. My 86-year-old father spent those days literally by her bedside, keeping watch over his bride of sixty-three years. One morning I received a call informing me that my dad had suffered a major stroke. The nurses had come in and found him in my mom's room, slumped over in a chair.

We quickly made the one-hundred-mile journey from our home in Chehalis, Washington to Newberg, Oregon and found our way into dad's hospital room. Now, both of my parents were patients in the same hospital, and although we did not know it at the time, they would never return to their home on the farm again. Dad was unresponsive, and the doctors said within twenty-four hours we would know the extent of the damage from the stroke.

As our family sat around his bed, we spoke softly and lovingly to my father, but there was no response—no open eyes to acknowledge our presence and no words to answer ours. After spending some time speaking to him, reminiscing, praying and reading Scripture, our youngest daughter Jana suggested we sing to Grandpa. He had taught her many old hymns when she was a child, and it was fitting for her to sing to Grandpa at this time.

As Jana began to sing and we joined with her, something unexpected occurred. My comatose father, who had showed no response whatsoever to any of our attempts to communicate, suddenly began to sing along. We were singing one of his favorite hymns, "The Old Rugged Cross," and he began singing in unison, knowing the words to every verse. His voice was weak at best, but it let us know he was still there. Then we sang "Amazing Grace." By the time we got to "When we've been there ten thousand years," there wasn't a dry eye among us.

We stopped singing and just wept in quiet amazement, knowing that we had just witnessed a miracle. Although the light wasn't on and it didn't appear that anyone was home, Dad was still there! Before we left, we prayed with him, and there was still no other physical sign of consciousness. How do you explain a comatose man with no outward signs of cognitive recognition, suddenly not only joining in a group activity, but singing on tune? Dr. Oliver Sachs, Harvard professor and psychiatrist, writes about this phenomenon in his interesting book *Musicophilia*. While he provides fascinating case studies and offers some scientific explanations for similar occurrences, I believe it goes deeper than science. Even though Dad's physical body was ravaged by the stroke and his mind showed no outward signs of engaging, there was something still living within the soul and spirit of the man. When we began to sing familiar lyrics and melodies, something stirred deep within his soul and spirit. Years of spiritual formation, familiarity with not only the lyrics of hymns, but the deeper meaning and relationship with God behind them, suddenly rose to the occasion. Despite the restraints of body and mind, we witnessed a triumph of the soul and spirit—the result of a lifetime of organic spiritual formation.

Dad did improve, although he never did regain his former vitality, and within six months both my mother and father passed from this life. None of us who were there will ever forget that moment when something within Dad's spirit caused him to sing those familiar words to songs that had meant so much to him in his lifetime. But as wonderful as that miracle was, it was only temporary at best. The much greater miracle is our hope that both my mother and father are alive and well in heaven because of authentic faith in the Lord Jesus Christ. That faith was passed on to me, and I am forever grateful. That faith helps us navigate and grow organically through all the seasons of life.

Reflection Questions for Pastors and Church Leaders

1. After reading through this book, what are your thoughts about organic spiritual formation? Has your church taken a more programmatic approach to discipleship and evangelism, and if so, how is it working for you?

2. How could some of the organic principles of growth be applied in your local church setting?

3. If you were to do a spiritual health examination for your parishioners, how would they score? Do you think most are growing in their faith, or do they feel stuck? What would it take to actually survey your people and discover the answers?

4. If your church has specific mission, purpose, or core value statements, why not ask participants in your next board meeting or leadership team meeting to recite them from memory? If key leaders are unable to do so, what might that be telling you? If they are able to do so, what does that say? Is there alignment between those statements and your actual practices and outcomes?

5. What traditions within your church organizational structure or environment hinder growth in evangelism and discipleship? What traditions are helpful anchors to the past?

6. How many new believers have been baptized or become members of your church over the past year? Are you happy

with those results? How does that number correspond with the number of decisions to follow Christ?

7. Is it possible that some of those who make commitments to Christ feel like orphans in terms of having someone to personally mentor them and nurture their spiritual growth?

8. Do you have any type of intentional process for nurturing new believers toward becoming fully developed followers of Jesus Christ? If so, what does it look like and can you clearly articulate it?

9. Do your parishioners feel comfortable inviting their unchurched or unbelieving friends to accompany them to your services? Have you ever asked that question? What might the answers tell you?

10. How do you incorporate the work of the Holy Spirit into everything you do as a church, including corporate worship, evangelism, and discipleship?

11. Is prayer a priority in your church? What are some ways you might incorporate prayer into fellowship and other life/community events to become more natural and organic?

12. Are you telling stories of life change and growth within both your larger church corporate settings and small group settings?

12. As Pastor Wayne Cordeiro tells us in the title of his book, *Jesus, Plain and Simple*, how plainly and simply is Jesus presented to both visitors and members of your church? Are you satisfied with your answer?

13. Even if you are a relatively new congregation planted in the last decade, you may be discovering that along with growth comes encroaching bureaucracy, fundraising priorities to meet budgets, and more corporate structures. Perhaps these are the very issues you hoped to avoid when you first began.

How can you keep things more organic and prevent your own traditions and encroaching bureaucracy from taking you off mission?

14. How is your church living out the Great Commission and mission of God? What do you think about the idea of aligning the Great Commission components with the simple concepts of going, showing, growing, and knowing?

15. Where will you go from here in providing tools and resources for people to grow in a more organic fashion as they mature into fully developed followers of Jesus Christ?

Notes

PREFACE

1. Excerpted from *The American Heritage Dictionary of the English Language, Third Edition* (New York: Houghton Mifflin Company, 1996).

2. William Dietrich, "Satisfying an Old Hunger," *The Seattle Times Footprint Pacific Northwest Extra*, September 28, 2009, 12–13.

3. David Kinnaman, *You Lost Me*, Kindle Edition (Grand Rapids, Mich.: Baker Books, 2011) locations 511–513.

CHAPTER ONE: A SPIRITUAL HEALTH EXAMINATION

1. Sonia Krishnan, "Beyond Potlucks," *The Seattle Times*, July 29, 2007, online at http://seattletimes.nwsource.com/html/pacificnw07292007/2003802221_pacificpgrange29.html.

2. Ibid.

3. Christine Wicker, "How Spiritual Are We?" *Parade*, October 4, 2009, 4–5.

4. Charts are from the *Reveal Survey* from Willow Creek Association, available online at www.revealnow.com and used by permission from Willow Creek Association.

5. Willow Creek Association advertisement for *Reveal* at http://www.willowcreek.com/wca_prod.asp?invtid=PR30332&section=books, accessed 4/15/09.

6. Greg L. Hawkins, Cally Parkinson, *Follow Me: What's Next For You?* (Barrington, Ill.: Willow Creek Publishing, 2008), 103.

7. Greg L. Hawkins, Cally Parkinson, *Move: What 1,000 Churches Reveal About Spiritual Growth* (Grand Rapids, Mich.: Zondervan, 2011), 26.

8. Ibid., 24.

9. Data from office of Statistician, General Council Assemblies of God, Springfield, Missouri (accessed May, 2012).

CHAPTER FOUR: BASIC ELEMENTS OF FAITH

1. John Ortberg, "Your Spiritual Growth Plan," *Leadership*, Winter 2010, 81.

2. Ibid.

3. Frank Hobbs, Nicole Stoops, *Demographic Trends in the 20th Century* (Washington, D.C.: United States Census Bureau, 2002), 7.

4. "Historical Timeline—Farmers & the Land," on educational website, *Growing a Nation: The Story of American Agriculture,* http://www.agclassroom.org/gan/timeline/farmers_land.htm.

CHAPTER SEVEN: GOOD NUTRITION FUELS GROWTH

1. Nanci Helmich, "Obesity a key link to soaring health tab as costs double," *USA Today*, October 7, 2009, http://www.usatoday.com/news/health/2009-07-27-costofobesity_N.htm?csp=DailyBriefing.

2. James Dalton Morrison, ed., *Masterpieces of Religious Verse* (New York: Harper, 1948). Also included in *Poems that Touch the Heart,* compiled by A.L. Alexander (New York: Doubleday, 1941, 1956).

3. "Mapping the Global Muslim Population," *Pew Forum on Religion and Public Life* (Washington, D.C.: Pew Research Center Publications, October 8, 2009), http://pewresearch.org/pubs/1370/mapping-size-distribution-worlds-muslim-population.

4. Anup Shau, "Poverty Stats and Facts," (*Global Issues*, March 22, 2009), updated at http://www.globalissues.org/article/26/poverty-facts-and-stats.

CHAPTER EIGHT: STRUGGLES GROW COURAGE AND CHARACTER

1. C.H. Spurgeon (compiled by Al Bryant), *Day by Day with C.H. Spurgeon: A Sourcebook of Daily Meditations from the "Prince of Preachers"* (Grand Rapids, Mich.: Kregel, 1980, 1992), 63–64.

CHAPTER NINE: SEASONS PROVIDE THE RHYTHM OF LIFE

1. Henri Nouwen, *The Inner Voice of Love* (New York: Doubleday, 1996), 31.

2. Herbert A. Applebaum, *The American Work Ethic and the Changing Work Force* (Westport, Conn.: Greenwood Press, 1998), 157.

3. William Shakespeare, *Macbeth*, Act 1, Scene 1, Line 58.

CHAPTER TEN: SPIRITUAL FORMATION REQUIRES A JOURNEY

1. J.R. Kerr, "Open Source Activists," *Leadershipjournal.net*, October 6, 2009, http://www.christianitytoday.com/le/buildingleaders/equipping/opensourceactivists.html.

CHAPTER THIRTEEN: TEAMWORK MAKES HARVEST POSSIBLE

1. Eugene Peterson, *Eat This Book* (Grand Rapids, Mich.: William B. Eerdmans, 2006), 70–71; paraphrased in the

September 18 entry of *Men of Integrity* (September/October 2009), http://www.christianitytoday.com/moi/.

2. William Engle, "God is my Landlord," *The American Weekly*, 1949. Reprinted in *Good Old Days*, December 1996, 33, 53–54.

3. Richard Foster, "Spiritual Formation Agenda," *Christianity Today*, January 2009, 29–33.

For further information and discussion visit:
www.growingorganicdisciples.com
You can find Don Detrick on Facebook and Twitter (@dondetrick)
www.dondetrick.com